Christ Sutras

Bart Marshall

Christ Sutras

The Complete Sayings of Jesus Christ
From All Sources
Arranged into Sermons

Illustrated with portraits of Jesus of Nazareth
by Rembrandt van Rijn

Bart Marshall

REALFACE PRESS

Published by Realface Press
www.realfacepress.com

First Edition November 2015

Cover art: *Christ with Arms Folded*, Rembrandt van Rijn

Ask and it shall be given you.
Seek and you shall find.
Knock and it shall be opened to you.

For everyone who asks receives,
and he who seeks finds.
and to him who knocks, it will be opened.

For the one who speaks is also the one who hears,
and the one who sees is also the one who manifests,
and the one who seeks is also the one who reveals.

Let him who seeks continue seeking until he finds.
When he finds, he will become troubled,
and when he becomes troubled he will be astonished,
and he will rule over the All.

Table of Contents

Introduction

There was a game, you may remember, that schoolteachers had us play as kids where a person at one corner of the classroom whispers a sentence to the next person, who whispers it to the next person and so on until it is whispered to the last person, who says out loud what he thought he heard in his ear. The teacher then reads the original sentence, which of course bears little resemblance to what the last person thought was said.

The words of Jesus have no doubt suffered a similar fate, passing through decades, even centuries, of ears and minds before being written down. Yet miraculously, the essence of his teachings has survived, and contained within the sayings attributed to Jesus Christ are some of the most profound and moving pointers to Truth ever voiced.

After his death, the words and teachings of Jesus lived on in a diverse and vibrant oral tradition. Sects formed around different aspects or interpretations of the teachings, and over the next few hundred years, thousands of manuscripts appeared claiming to contain the words and teachings of Jesus, each emphasizing and embellishing those aspects most important to the writer and the sect to which he belonged. There were arguments between sects, of course, as to which among them should be considered the true church, and over time several powerful contenders emerged.

Not surprisingly, the group backed by the Roman emperor eventually came out on top. In 325 AD they convened a council at Nicaea and declared themselves the one and only Christian Church. They issued a creed specifying official Church beliefs, and from the thousands of Christian writings in circulation, chose twenty-seven to become the approved canon, the New Testament. The rest became *apocrypha*, from the Greek, meaning, "those left out." Most of these writings were declared heretical by the new Church and many were ordered destroyed. Sects that taught an aspect of Christianity in conflict with official Church doctrine were forced underground.

Copies of some apocrypha texts have survived, mostly in fragments, but they are still largely ignored by the modern Church. Interest in apocrypha texts among individuals, however, both Christian and non-Christian, has increased dramatically in recent decades, due mainly to the discovery of thirteen leather-bound papyrus codices found buried in a cave near Nag Hammadi, Egypt in 1945. The wife of the farmer who discovered them burned one of the codices as fuel for cooking, but twelve survive, containing over fifty ancient Christian texts. Now popularly known as the Gnostic Gospels, these books, The Gospel of Thomas chief among them, have become the focal point for a new examination of the essential teachings of Christ. In them are sayings that exhort us as individuals to experience directly the Truth of God for ourselves, and thus become a Christ, a Son of God.

Interestingly, once we see this teaching expressed more clearly in some of the apocrypha, it is easier to see that it can be found throughout the New Testament as well. Christian mystics like Saint John of the Cross and Meister Eckhart experienced first hand the truth of this teaching, and wrote about the wonder of discovering that, as Eckhart puts it, "The eye with which I see God is the same eye with which God sees me." Or as Jesus says, "He who knows himself, at the same time knows the Totality of the All."

This is the teaching that drew me to the project that has become *Christ Sutras*. It started while I was working on *The Perennial Way*, a collection of new translations of ancient eastern texts on enlightenment. I realized that nothing like these works existed for Jesus—nothing like the *Dhammapada* of Buddha, for instance, that contained Jesus' words alone in an organized, poetic arrangement. The more I thought about the lack of such a resource the more I felt the need of it and, well, one thing led to another.

My initial idea was to arrange selected sayings of Jesus into a *Dhammapada*-like sermon, a composition of *sutras*, that encapsulated his highest teachings in a fluid, hopefully moving, narrative. I realized that to do this I would first need to assemble all of his sayings in order to make my choices. When the question of what constituted *all* arose, it pretty much answered itself. All means all.

Certainly there are those who believe that only the New Testament should be consulted in these matters, but when we read in the Gospel of John that if every great thing Jesus said and did were recorded "even the whole world would not have room for the books that would be written," we find ourselves wishing we had more, not less. Ignoring much of what *was* written based on the decrees of imperfect men in a distant millennia seems counter-intuitive.

Ultimately, of course, there is no way to prove or disprove whether Jesus said everything that's been attributed to him, or even any of it. But regardless, a tremendous wealth of powerful sayings attributed to Jesus has survived for our consideration—a gift whose origin is in many ways inconsequential.

And so for *Christ Sutras* I adopted the criteria of gathering from all the surviving Christian texts thought to have been in circulation at the time the books for the New Testament were chosen, including, of course, the canonical gospels. Twenty-five surviving texts from this time period contain quotes attributed to Jesus. Five are in the New Testament, twenty are not.

The next step, choosing which sayings I thought represented Jesus' highest teachings, proved more difficult than I imagined. I also began to see that I was taking upon myself a role not unlike the Church Fathers who decreed what we should read and not read in regards to Jesus. I realized then that my opinions were of little consequence, and that it was much more important to present all of Jesus' teachings as an uncensored, unified whole so that individuals might discern the truth or untruth of each saying for themselves, personally and directly. And so I used all the extant sayings of Jesus to create forty-one sermons, each expounding on a different topic in a fluid narrative.

The sermons are organized into seven chapters. Chapter I: "Inner Teachings," includes sermons that expound on the more esoteric topics that Jesus may have reserved for those with "ears to hear." As he says, "It is to those who are worthy of my mysteries that I tell my mysteries. "

The sermons in Chapter II: "Discipleship," contain teachings describing the life of commitment required of those who choose to follow the Way of Jesus. Chapter III: "Wandering Prophet," and Chapter IV: "Parables and Metaphors," consist of sermons suitable for the multitudes, as well as close followers.

Chapter V: "Destiny," comprises sermons and teachings concerning the last days of Jesus, leading up to and including crucifixion and resurrection.

The sermons in Chapter VI: "Prophesy," embrace the darker side of Jesus' teachings, and speak in depth of war, apocalypse, judgment and damnation. Chapter VII: "Cosmology," contains highly metaphysical sermons composed almost exclusively from sayings found in Gnostic gospels.

Because *Christ Sutras* contains the full measure of Christ's sayings, what emerges is a more richly textured teaching than that of the New Testament alone. Some readers may decide to choose which sayings they can accept, and thus the Christ they can accept. Others may look for a place within themselves where Christ Consciousness might contain and find occasion to speak all these things.

There is no right or wrong in this. Whatever one may ultimately accept or not accept of these sayings is not nearly as important as the self-honesty, introspection and intuition we must call upon as we reflect on them.

As a footnote, what you surrender is often returned. In the end, after all the sermons were completed and I was putting the finishing touches on the appendices, I was unexpectedly reminded of my original reason for undertaking this project, and in what felt like no more than a casual afterthought, that which I had given up was asked of me. The result is a 42nd sermon, "Book of Yeshua." It begins on page 221.

The codices discovered at Nag Hammadi in 1945

Editorial Notes

The sayings of Jesus collected in *Christ Sutras* have survived nearly two thousand years of translations, interpretations, misinterpretations and purgings, so my prime directive to myself when taking on this book was, "First do no [further] harm." I've been as faithful as possible to the original language of these sayings, as best can be determined from the earliest translations and many subsequent versions, and equally faithful to the teaching and intent of each verse. For the New Testament gospels, rather than choose a single Bible version to quote from, twenty-six versions of the Bible were consulted (Appendix A), looking for the "best of the best" version of each saying, often merging versions, so that *Christ Sutras* might contain the most faithful, readable versions of these sayings possible. For the apocrypha there exist far fewer translations and versions available, and in some cases those that exist are rough. For these my approach was to smooth out confusing grammar where needed, while being careful to preserve the integrity of the original.

In cases where the same saying or parable occurs in multiple sources, I combined them into a single complete version using all the details from each and cited multiple sources for those verses in the cross-reference table (Appendix B). Where including questions or words spoken by someone other than Jesus seemed necessary, they are shown in *italics*. To keep this to a minimum, in some *Christ Sutras* verses Jesus briefly paraphrases the question or situation as part of his response. In sayings where Jesus addresses a disciple by name, that name is often excluded so that the saying reads like Jesus speaking directly to all of us, which, of course, he is. The most challenging decisions arose when the selection of a word or phrase affected the meaning or connotation of a saying. In these cases I chose what most closely reflects the highest teachings of Christ as I understand them.

The conventions for capitalization differ widely in the many versions of the New Testament, as well as in the other texts. For *Christ Sutras* I adopted the convention of capitalizing everything that denotes a singularity, such as God, One, Christ, Son of Man, Heaven, and Hell. Also, certain common words are capitalized when used to denote a singularity greater than the generic usage of the word, such as Spirit, Light, Life, Truth, Way and Word. Except for a few instances, I chose not to capitalize pronouns referring to God or Jesus.

List of Illustrations

The paintings used as illustrations in *Christ Sutras* are by Rembrandt van Rijn (1606–1669) and his studio, most of them from an extraordinary series of very personal "portraits" of Jesus Christ.

When painting the face of Jesus in Rembrandt's day, artists were expected to draw upon three approved sources as their models: the Veil of Veronica, the Mandylion of Edessa, and the Lentulus Letters. These sources were considered sacred, therefore artists were instructed to

Self Portrait, Rembrandt van Rijn, Oil on canvas. English Heritage, Kenwood House, London

use them as guides in depicting Jesus' face. As a result, paintings of Jesus presented a stereotypic, mostly European image of Christ.

Rembrandt challenged this tradition by painting the face of Jesus "from life." The young man sitting for the portraits is thought to be a Sephardic Jew who settled in Amsterdam after being expelled from Spain, and whom Rembrandt found while searching his neighborhood for the right model for his project.

In the moving portraits that emerged, we see a powerful range of emotions in the face of Christ. While the traditional master paintings of Jesus tend to keep us at a distance, these radically intimate portraits invite us in, and leave us with the sense that we've seen more deeply into Jesus the man, and Jesus the Christ, than perhaps ever before.

Rembrandt apparently felt the same way about them. At the end of his life, bankrupt and bereft of other possessions, he still had two of these *Head of Christ* paintings hanging in his bedroom, and a third hidden in a bin of his studio.

The Paintings

Frontispiece   *Christ with Arms Folded*, Rembrandt van Rijn
Oil on canvas: 109.2 x 90.2 cm
The Hyde Collection, Glens Falls

Page 6   *Head of Christ*, Rembrandt van Rijn
Oil on oak panel: 25 x 21.5 cm
Staatliche Museen, Berlin

Page 10   *Head of Christ*, Rembrandt van Rijn
Oil on oak panel: 24 x 19 cm

Chapter I
Inner Teachings

The Father
Alpha and Omega
The Narrow Gate
The Way
The Blessed

The sayings attributed to Jesus represent teachings on at least three levels, or layers. The outer layer he spoke to the masses, using parables and references that anyone might understand. From the masses came those with a deeper interest, who followed him and asked questions. To these he gave more detailed instruction. To those who heard and understood on this level he imparted the inner teachings.

I shall give you what no eye has seen,
and what no ear has heard,
and what no hand has touched,
and what has never occurred to the human mind.

To those with "ears to hear" Jesus described a way to become like him, to become as he is. Not after death, but now, in this lifetime.

He who will drink from my mouth will become like me,
and I myself shall become he,
and the things that are hidden shall be revealed to him.

The inner teachings of Jesus share a deep similarity with the enlightenment teachings of Buddha and other eastern sages. To account for this, some scholars speculate that Jesus spent his twenties in India. Perhaps. But regardless, the more fundamental reason these teachings sound similar is because they arise from, and point to, the same Truth.

1. The Father

He Who Is, is ineffable.   1.1
No principle knows him, no authority, no subjection,
nor any creature from the foundation of the world until now,
except he alone, and anyone to whom he wills to reveal himself
through him who is from Infinite Light.
Forevermore, I offer this great Salvation.

He Who Is, is immortal and eternal, having never been born.   1.2
Everything that is born will perish.
He is unbegotten, having no beginning.
Everything that has a beginning has an end.

Because no one rules over him he has no name.   1.3
Whatever has a name is the creation of another.
He is unperceivable. He has no form.
Whatever has form is the creation of another.

He has a semblance of his own —   1.4
not like any you have perceived or thought —
but a strange semblance that surpasses all things
and is greater than the universe.
It looks to every side and sees itself from itself.

He is infinite and ever incomprehensible.   1.5
He is unchanging good.
He is faultless. He is timeless.
He is imperishable and has no likeness to anything.
He is eternally blessed.

He is not knowable, yet he ever knows himself.   1.6
He is immeasurable. He is untraceable.
He is perfect, having no defect.

He is called, "Father of the Universe."   1.7

2. Alpha and Omega

You ask how your end will be?
Have you discovered, then, the beginning,
that you look for the end?
Where the beginning is, there also is the end.

2.1

Blessed is he who abides in the ever-beginning.
He will know the end, and will not experience death.

2.2

Blessed is He Who Is — before everything comes into being.
For He Who Is, ever has been, and ever shall be.

2.3

You think you know me, and know where I come from?
I have not come of my own accord.
He who sends me is true, and him you do not know.
I know him, for I am of him, and it is he who sends me.

2.4

You believe the Messiah is coming, the one who is called Christ,
and that he will show you all things?
I say to you truly, I who speak to you am he.

2.5

Fear not. I am the first and the last, the living One.
I am he that lived and was dead, and behold,
I am alive forevermore. I hold the keys of Hell and death.

2.6

I am Alpha and Omega, the beginning and the end,
that which is, which was, and which is to come — the Almighty.

2.7

I have come from the One,
to sit on your couch and eat from your table.
I was given some things of the Father.

2.8

I am he who exists undivided.
He who is undivided is filled with light.
He who is divided is filled with darkness.

2.9

For the light of the body is the eye.
If, therefore, your eye is single, your whole body is light.

2.10

But if your eye is divided, being part darkness,   2.11
your whole body is darkness.
Take heed, therefore, that the light within you is not darkness.
For if the light that you are is darkness,
how great is that darkness.

You will see the Light—   2.12
brighter than light and more perfect than perfection—
and the Son will be perfected through the Light, the Father.

The Father is perfect.   2.13
The Son becomes perfect through death and resurrection.
Each accomplishment surpasses the other.
I am fully the right hand of the Father.
I am in him who accomplishes.

The Father called me Christ, that I might come to earth   2.14
and anoint with the oil of Life everyone who comes to me.
And he called me Jesus, that I might heal every sin
of the ignorant and give to men the Truth of God.

I am wholly in the Father and the Father in me,   2.15
after his image, after his form, after his power,
after his perfection and after his light.
I am both here and with him who sent me.
And I am his perfect Word.

I have received all power from the Father   2.16
that I may bring those in darkness into light,
those in corruptibility into incorruptibility,
those in error into righteousness,
those in captivity into freedom,
those in death into life.

For what is impossible on the part of men   2.17
is possible on the part of the Father.

I am the hope of the hopeless, the helper of those   2.18
who have no helper, the treasure of those in need,
the physician of the sick, and the resurrection of the dead.

Before Abraham was, I am.   2.19
All authority is given me, on earth and in Heaven.
I and the Father are One.

I came to make the things below like the things above,   2.20
and the things outside like those inside.
I came to unite them in that Place.

I am the Way, the Truth, and the Life.   2.21
All who come to the Father, come through me.
If you know me, you know the Father.
Henceforth you know him, and have seen him.

He who will drink from my mouth will become like me,   2.22
and I myself shall become he,
and the things that are hidden shall be revealed to him.

Inquire then, and I will tell you all you wish to know,   2.23
and I myself will make known to you what you do not ask.

"When will the repose of the dead come about,   2.24
and when will the new world come?"
I tell you, what you look forward to has already come,
but you do not recognize it.

When you see your likeness, you rejoice.   2.25
But when you see your image — that which came into being
before you, and which neither dies nor becomes manifest —
how much you will have to bear!

The image manifests into men, but the light in them   2.26
remains concealed in the image, in the Light of the Father.
The Father becomes manifest as men,
but his image remains concealed in his Light.

All natures, all forms, all creatures,   2.27
exist in and with one another, and they are resolved again
into their own roots. For the nature of matter is resolved
into the roots of its nature alone.

A great difference exists between the imperishable   2.28
and those who will perish.
Everything that comes from the perishable will perish,
for it comes from the perishable.
But whatever comes from the imperishable does not perish,
but itself becomes imperishable.

The multitude of men go astray   2.29
because they do not know this difference.
And they die.
Whoever has ears to hear about infinities, let him hear!
It is those who are awake that I address.
I come from the One that I might tell you all things.

It is to those who are worthy of my mysteries   2.30
that I tell my mysteries. Whoever finds the truth
of my words will not experience death.

There is light within a man of Light,   2.31
and he lights up the whole world.
If he does not shine, he is in darkness.
It is in Light that light exists.

I am the Light of the world.   2.32
He who becomes as me will not walk in darkness,
but will be the Light of Life.

He who becomes as me will also do the works that I do,   2.33
and greater works than these will he do.

I shall give you what no eye has seen,   2.34
and what no ear has heard, and what no hand has touched,
and what has never occurred to the human mind.

Heaven and earth will roll up in your presence.   2.35
For whoever finds himself, contains the world.

Take heed of the Living One while you are alive,   2.36
lest you die and seek to know him but be unable to do so.
He who lives from the Living One will not see death.

It is I who am the Light above the All.
It is I who am the All.
From me does the All come forth.
Into me does the All extend.

Split a piece of wood and I am there.
Lift up a stone and you will find me.

2.37

2.38

3. The Narrow Gate

Enter by the narrow gate.
For wide is the gate and broad is the way
that leads to destruction.
And there are many who go in by it.

3.1

But strait is the gate and narrow is the path
that leads to Life.
And there are few who find it.

3.2

Recognize what is in your sight,
and that which is hidden will become plain to you.
For there is nothing hidden that will not become manifest.

3.3

Come to hate falsehood and the evil of thought.
For it is thought that gives birth to falsehood,
and falsehood is far from Truth.

3.4

Ask and it shall be given you.
Seek and you shall find.
Knock and it shall be opened to you.

3.5

For everyone who asks receives,
and he who seeks finds,
and to him who knocks, it will be opened.

3.6

For the one who speaks is also the one who hears,
and the one who sees is also the one who manifests,
and the one who seeks is also the one who reveals.

3.7

Let him who seeks continue seeking until he finds.
When he finds, he will become troubled,
and when he becomes troubled he will be astonished,
and he will reign over the All.

3.8

While you yet have time in the world, listen to me,
and I will reveal to you the things you ponder in your mind.

3.9

You are my twin and true companion.   3.10
Examine yourself that you may understand who you are,
in what way you exist, and how you come to be.

You are my twin, my brother.   3.11
It is not fitting that you be ignorant of yourself.
I know that you understand, because you already perceive
that I am the knowledge of Truth.

So while you accompany me, although you appear   3.12
uncomprehending, you have in fact already come to know,
and you are indeed, "One who knows himself."

He who does not know himself knows nothing.   3.13
But he who knows himself,
at the same time knows the Totality of the All.

So it is that you, my brother, behold that which is obscure   3.14
to men, and against which they ignorantly stumble.

Blessed are the eyes that see the things you see.   3.15
For many prophets and kings have desired
to see what you see and have not seen it,
to hear what you hear and have not heard it.

I know that in faith and with your whole heart   3.16
you question me. Therefore I am glad because of you.
I am truly pleased, and my Father in me rejoices
that you thus inquire and ask.
Your boldness makes me rejoice, and it affords you Life.

That which you have within you will save you   3.17
if you bring it forth from yourself.
That which you do not have within you will kill you
if you do not have it within you.

Wretched is the person who depends on a body.   3.18
Wretched is the soul that depends on these two.
Woe to the flesh that depends on the soul.
Woe to the soul that depends on the flesh.

The enjoyment of this world is a lie,
and its gold and its silver is error.
Whoever seeks Life knows this. This is their wealth.

3.19

I laugh at this world not only because it is a trifle,
but because I am full of contempt for it.
Whoever comes to know the world finds only a corpse.
Whoever finds the corpse is superior to the world.

3.20

When you leave behind the things that cannot follow you,
then you will know peace. He who truly wants
to enter the kingdom of Heaven, will enter it.

3.21

Whoever would become as me, let him deny himself.
Let him take up his cross and follow me.
For whoever would save his life will lose it,
but whoever loses his life for my sake, will save it.
What shall it profit a man if he gain the whole world,
yet lose his own soul?

3.22

Truly, he who loves his life shall lose it.
But he who renounces his life in this world,
shall know eternal Life.

3.23

Have faith and be of good courage.
Truly I say to you, such a rest will be yours,
where there is no eating, nor drinking, nor mourning,
nor singing, nor care, nor earthly garment, nor death.

3.24

You will no longer have your part in the lesser creation,
but will belong to the incorruptibility of the Father,
and you will not perish.

3.25

For you are in Christ always,
and Christ is always in the Father.

3.26

If those who lead you say, "The kingdom of God is in the sky,"
then the birds of the sky will precede you. If they say to you,
"It is in the sea," then the fish will precede you.
Rather, the kingdom of God is inside you, and before you.

3.27

When you come to know yourself,   3.28
you will become what is known, and you will realize
that you are the son of the living Father.

But if you do not know yourself, you dwell in poverty,   3.29
and it is you who are that poverty.
For whoever believes he is less than the All,
is completely ignorant.

The kingdom of God is when the two become one,   3.30
when that which is without is as that which is within,
when the male and the female are neither male nor female.

For when you make the two, one, you become a son of God. 3.31
And when you say, "Mountain, move away,"
it will move away.

To enter the Kingdom, become like an infant.   3.32
For when you make the two, one,
and make the inside like the outside,
and make the outside like the inside,
and make the above like the below,
and when you make the male and female one and the same,
so that the male not be male, nor the female be female,
and when you fashion an eye in place of an eye,
and a hand in place of a hand, and a foot in place of a foot,
and a likeness in place of a likeness,
then will you enter the kingdom of God.

The kingdom of God is not found by looking out.   3.33
No one can tell you, "Look here," or "Look there."
The kingdom of God is within you.

The Kingdom will not come by waiting for it.   3.34
It will not be a matter of saying, "I found it," or "There it is."
The kingdom of God is everywhere but you do not see it!

This heaven will pass away, and the ones above it   3.35
will pass away. The dead are not alive
and the living will not die.

When you consume what is dead, you make it what is alive. 3.36
When you come to dwell in the light, what will you do?
In the day when you were One, you became two.
But when you come to see you are two, what will you do?

Unless you are born anew, you cannot enter the Kingdom. 3.37
Unless you are born of water and spirit,
you cannot see the kingdom of God.
That which is born of the flesh is flesh.
That which is born of spirit is spirit.

Do not marvel that I say, "You must be born anew." 3.38
The wind blows where it will and you hear the sound of it,
but you do not know whence it comes or whither it goes.
So it is with everyone who is born of Spirit.

Therefore let these children come to me, do not hinder them, 3.39
for they behold the kingdom of God.
Whoever receives one such child in my name receives me.
Whoever receives me, receives not me,
but Him whom I am from.

Truly, whoever does not receive the kingdom of God 3.40
as an infant child does, cannot enter it.

4. The Way

Seek and you shall find.
Knock and it shall be opened to you.

4.1

What you asked me about in former times,
and which I did not tell you then, I now desire to tell.
Yet you do not inquire after it.

4.2

While you are elated at the promise of Life, are you still sad?
Do you grieve when you are instructed in the Kingdom?

4.3

You, through faith and knowledge, have received Life.
Therefore disdain the rejection when you hear it,
and when you hear the promise, rejoice the more.

4.4

Truly, he who receives Life and enters the Kingdom
will never leave it. Not even the Father can banish him.

4.5

He who glorifies the Father is the dwelling of the Father.
He who is of God, hears the word of God.
The reason you do not hear God, is that you are not of God.

4.6

What must you do to be doing the work of God, the Father?
The work of God is to become as him he sends to you.

4.7

O ye of little faith, how long yet do you ask me,
and inquire only without anguish after what you wish to hear?

4.8

Keep my commandments and follow my Way,
without reserve, without delay, without respect of persons.
Walk the straight, direct, and narrow path,
and in every respect the Father will rejoice concerning you.

4.9

Take my yoke upon you and learn from me.
I am gentle and humble in heart,
and you will find rest for your souls.
My yoke is easy, and my burden is light.

4.10

Come, follow me. I will make you fishers of men.
Come, follow me. Let the dead bury their dead.

4.11

He who knows and keeps my commandments loves me.
He who loves me will be loved by my Father,
and I will love him, and manifest myself to him.

4.12

And if you ask anything in my name, I will do it.
If you love me, therefore, keep my commandments.

4.13

The Lord your God is One. You shall love the Lord your God
with all your heart, and with all your soul,
and with all your mind, and with all your strength.
This is the first and greatest commandment.

4.14

You shall not tempt the Lord your God.
You shall worship the Lord your God,
and him only shall you serve.

4.15

The second commandment is like it:
Love your neighbor as yourself.
No commandment is greater than these.
On these two commandments
hang all the law and the prophets.

4.16

As I love you, therefore, love one another.
By this all men will know you are my disciples,
that you love one another.

4.17

Love your brother like your soul.
Guard him like the pupil of your eye.

4.18

Do not tell lies. Do not do what you hate.
For all things are plain in the vision of Heaven.
Nothing hidden will remain unmanifest.
Nothing covered will not be uncovered.

4.19

Do not labor for the food that perishes,
but for the food that endures to eternal Life,
that which the Son of Man will give to you.
For on him has God the Father set his seal.

4.20

Do not worry about your life,   4.21
about what you will eat or what you will drink,
nor about your body, about what clothing you will put on.
Do not be concerned from morning until evening,
and from evening until morning about what you will wear.

Is not life more than food and the body more than clothing?   4.22
Look at the birds of the air.
They neither sow nor reap nor gather into barns,
yet your Father in Heaven feeds them.
Are you not of more value than they?

Therefore, give no thought for tomorrow.   4.23
Let tomorrow come with tomorrow's things.
Sufficient for the day is its own arising.

Which of you by worrying can add one inch to his stature?   4.24
So why do you worry about clothing?
Consider the lilies of the field, how they grow.
They neither toil or spin, yet not even Solomon in all his glory
was arrayed like one of these.

Now if God so clothes the grass of the field,   4.25
which today is, and tomorrow is thrown into the oven,
will he not much more clothe you, O ye of little faith?

Therefore do not worry, saying, "What shall we eat?"   4.26
or "What shall we drink?" or "What shall we wear?"
These are the things sought by the mass of men.
Your Father in Heaven knows that you need these things.

Seek ye first the kingdom of God and his righteousness,   4.27
and all these things shall be added unto you.

Love your enemies. Do good to those who hate you.   4.28
Bless those who curse you.
Pray for those who spitefully use you.

To him who strikes you on one cheek, turn the other to him.   4.29
To him who takes your cloak, offer him your tunic.

Give to everyone who asks, and from him who
borrows your goods, do not ask for them back.

As you want men to do to you, do to them likewise.   4.30
If you love only those who love you,
what reward do you deserve?
Even tax collectors love those who love them.
And if you greet your brethren only,
what do you do more than others?
Do not even tax collectors greet their brethren?

If you do good to those who do good to you,   4.31
what credit is that to you? Even sinners do the same.
If you lend to those from whom you hope to receive back,
what credit is that to you?
Even sinners lend to sinners to receive as much back.

You must become perfect,   4.32
just as your Father in Heaven is perfect.

Take heed and beware of covetousness,   4.33
for one's life does not consist in the abundance
of the things he possesses.

Sell what you have and give alms.   4.34
Provide yourself moneybags that do not grow old.
Do not lay up for yourself treasures on earth,
where moth and rust destroy, where thieves break in and steal.

Lay up for yourself a treasure in Heaven that does not fail,   4.35
where neither moth nor rust destroys,
where thieves do not break in and steal.
For where your treasure is, there will your heart be also.

What man is there among you who,   4.36
if his son asks for bread, would give him a stone?
Or if he asks for a fish, would give him a serpent?
Or if he asks for an egg, would give him a scorpion?

If you then, being ignorant,   4.37
know how to give good gifts to your children,

how much more will your Father in Heaven
give good gifts to those who ask?
He will give the gift of the Holy Spirit to those who ask him!

Whatever you want men to do to you, do also to them.   4.38
This is the law and the prophets.

When you pray, be not like the hypocrites.   4.39
They love to pray standing in the synagogues
and on the corners of streets, that they may be seen by men.
Assuredly, I say to you, that is their only reward.

But you, when you pray, go into your room,   4.40
shut the door behind you, and pray to your Father in secret.
Your Father, who sees in secret, will reward you openly.

And when you pray, do not use vain repetitions   4.41
as the heathen do. They think they will be heard
for their many words. Do not be like them.
Your Father knows the things you need before you ask him.

Do not be like the Pharisee in the temple, who prayed: 4.42
"God, I thank you that I am not like other men —
extortionists, adulterers, or even like that tax collector.
I fast twice a week. I give tithes of all that I possess."

Be like that tax collector praying afar off in the temple,   4.43
who did not so much as raise his eyes to the heavens,
but beat his breast, saying, "God, be merciful to me a sinner!"
Truly, this man went home justified rather than the other.

For he who exalts himself will be humbled,   4.44
and he who humbles himself will be exalted.

Do not do your charitable deeds before men   4.45
in order to be seen and praised by them. If you do,
you shall have no reward from your Father in Heaven.

When you do a charitable deed, do not sound a trumpet   4.46
before you as the hypocrites do in the synagogues

and the streets, that they may have glory from men.
Assuredly, it will be their only reward.

Rather, when you do a charitable deed,   4.47
let not your left hand know what your right hand is doing.
Let your charitable deed be done in secret.
Your Father, who sees in secret, will reward you openly.

Listen: A certain man was travelling from Jerusalem to Jericho   4.48
and fell among thieves who stripped him of his clothing,
wounded him and departed, leaving him half dead.

Now by chance a certain priest came down that road.   4.49
And when he saw him he passed by on the other side.
Likewise a Levite, when he arrived at that place
came and looked, then passed by on the other side.

But a Samaritan, as he journeyed, came to where he was.   4.50
And when he saw him he had compassion.
So he went to him and bandaged his wounds,
pouring on oil and wine, and set him on his own animal.

He brought him to an inn, and took care of him.   4.51
The next day as he departed, he gave the innkeeper two denarii
and said, "Take care of this man, and whatever more it costs,
I will pay you when I come again."

So which of these three was neighbor to him who fell   4.52
among the thieves? He who showed mercy, certainly.
Go and do likewise.

And when you give a feast do not ask your friends,   4.53
your brothers, your relatives, nor rich neighbors,
lest they invite you back and you be repaid.

When you give a feast invite the poor,   4.54
the lame, the maimed and the blind.
You will be blessed because they cannot repay you.
You shall be repaid at the resurrection of the just.

And when someone invites you to a feast,   4.55
do not sit in the best place, lest one more honorable
than you arrive, and he who invited you
come say to you, "Give your place to this man."
And with shame you then take a lower place.

Rather, when you are invited, sit in the lowest place,   4.56
so that he who invited you may come and say to you,
"Friend, go up higher." Then you will have glory
in the presence of those who sit at the table with you.

For truly, he who exalts himself will be humbled,   4.57
and he who humbles himself will be exalted.

And when you fast, do not be like the hypocrites,   4.58
who fast with a sad countenance. They contort their faces
so they may appear to men to be fasting.
Assuredly, I say to you, they have their reward.

But you, when you fast, anoint your head and wash your face   4.59
so that you do not appear to men to be fasting,
but only to your Father, who is in the secret place.
Your Father, who sees in secret, will reward you openly.

If you have money, do not lend it at interest.   4.60
Give it to one from whom you will not get it back.
Do good and give, hoping for nothing in return.
Your reward will be great, and you will be a son of God.
God is kind also to the ignorant and unthankful.

Be merciful, just as your Father is merciful.   4.61
Judge not, that you not be judged.
Condemn not, that you not be condemned.
Let he who is without sin cast the first stone.
Love your enemies.

For with what judgment you judge, you shall be judged,   4.62
and the measure you give will be the measure you get,
and still more will be given you.

Forgive, and you will be forgiven.   4.63
Give, and it will be given to you.
Good measure, pressed down, shaken together
and running over will be put into your bosom.

For if you forgive men their trespasses,   4.64
your Father in Heaven will also forgive you.
But if you do not forgive men their trespasses,
neither will your Father forgive your trespasses.

You see the mote in your brother's eye but you do not consider   4.65
the beam in your own eye. How can you say to your brother,
"Let me remove the mote from your eye,"
when, behold there is a beam in your own eye. Hypocrite!
Remove the beam from your own eye, so that you see clearly.
Then you can remove the mote from your brother's eye.

If you see with your own eyes how your brother sins,   4.66
then correct him, you alone. If he listens to you,
then you have won him. But if he does not listen to you,
then come out with one, or at most two others.
Correct your brother. But if even then he does not listen,
let him be to you as a heathen and a tax collector.

But if you only hear something,   4.67
do not accept any belief against your brother,
and do not slander, and do not love to listen to slander.
For it is written, "Let your ear listen to nothing
against your brother, but only if you have seen yourself,
then censure, correct and convert him."

Among those who believe in the teaching of my Word,   4.68
should there be dissension and dispute,
envy and confusion, hatred and distress?
You shall reprove one another and not regard the person,
and not hate the one who has corrected you.

Therefore, take heed to yourselves.   4.69
If your brother sins against you, rebuke him.
Tell him his fault between you and him alone.
If he hears you, you have gained your brother.

And if he repents, forgive him. And if he sins against you
seven times in a day, and seven times in a day returns to you,
saying, "I repent," forgive him.

But if he will not hear, take with you one or two more,
so that, "By the mouth of two or three witnesses
every word may be confirmed."

If he refuses to hear them, tell it to the church.
But if he refuses even to hear the church,
let him be to you like a heathen and a tax collector.

And if someone should fall bearing his burden,
such as committing a sin against his neighbor,
then his neighbor should admonish him as a service
for the good it will do for his neighbor.

And if he repents when his neighbor has admonished him,
he will be saved, and he who admonished him
will obtain eternal Life.

But if instead he argues how his neighbor
who renders him this service also sins,
and encourages him to sin,
such a one will be judged in a great judgment.
When a blind man leads a blind man, both fall into a ditch.

For the one who encourages and regards the person, and also
the one who is encouraged and whose person is regarded,
will both be punished with one punishment.

As the prophet said, "Woe to those who encourage the sinner
whose God is his belly, and speak fair to him
for the sake of a bribe." You see how the Judgment is?
Truly I say to you, in the day of Judgment
I will not fear the rich nor have pity for the poor.

I have given you an example,
that you also should do as I have done to you.
A servant is not greater than his master.
Nor is he who is sent greater than he who sent him.

4.70

4.71

4.72

4.73

4.74

4.75

4.76

4.77

4.78

Blessed are you if you know these things.
Blessed indeed are you if you live them.

For whoever hears these sayings of mine, and does them,   4.79
is like the wise man who built his house on the rock.
And when the rain descended, and the floods came,
and the winds blew and beat on that house,
it did not fall, for it was founded on the rock.

But whoever hears these sayings of mine and does not   4.80
do them, is like the foolish man who built his house on sand.
And when the rain descended, and the floods came,
and the winds blew and beat on that house, it fell.
And great was its fall.

Whoever breaks even the least of these commandments   4.81
and causes others to break them,
shall be called least in the kingdom of Heaven.

Whoever keeps these commandments   4.82
and teaches them to others,
shall be called great in the kingdom of Heaven.

Once more I prevail upon you, for I am here,   4.83
building a house that is of great value to you.
You will find shelter within it,
and it will stand firm when your neighbor's house falls.

No one will ever enter the kingdom of Heaven at my bidding,   4.84
but only because you yourself are whole.
Hearken to the Word, understand Knowledge, love Life.
No one persecutes or oppresses you other than you yourself!

I have many more things to tell you,   4.85
but you cannot bear them now. When the Spirit of Truth
comes to you, he will guide you into all the Truth.

He will not speak to you on his own authority, but whatever   4.86
he hears from me he will speak, and he will declare to you
the things that are to come. He will glorify me,
for he will take what is mine and give it to you.

Everything I have said to you,   4.87
you have heard and received in faith.
If you know these things for yourself, they are yours.
If you do not know them for yourself, they are not yours.

Hasten to be saved without being urged!   4.88
Be eager of your own accord and, if possible,
arrive even before me. Your Father will love you.

See rightly! The kingdom of Heaven is within you!   4.89

5. The Blessed

Blessed are the humble in spirit, for theirs is the kingdom of God. 5.1
Blessed are those who weep, for they shall laugh.
Blessed are those who mourn, for they shall be comforted.
Blessed are those who hunger and thirst for righteousness,
for the belly of he who desires shall be filled.

Blessed are the merciful, for they shall obtain mercy. 5.2
Blessed are the pure in heart, for they shall see God.
Blessed are those without pride, for they shall inherit the earth.
Blessed are those who find peace within themselves,
for they shall become sons of God.

And blessed are you 5.3
when men hate and revile and persecute you,
and say all manner of evil against you because you love God.
Rejoice in that day and be exceedingly glad,
for great is your reward in Heaven.
So did men persecute the prophets before you,
and whoever persecutes you will find no Place.

Yet blessed are they who are persecuted within themselves. 5.4
It is they who truly come to know the Father.

Blessed are the solitary and the elect, 5.5
for they will find the kingdom of God.
You are from it, and to it you will return.

Blessed are you who do not waver at the sight of me, 5.6
for where the mind is, there is the treasure.

Blessed are you who weep and are oppressed by those 5.7
without hope, for you will be released from every bondage.

Blessed are you who have knowledge 5.8
of the stumbling blocks, and who escape adverse forces.

Blessed are you who hear the Word of God and keep it. 5.9
Blessed are you who suffer and find Life.

Chapter II

Discipleship

Son of Man
Brethren
The Female
Prayer
Going Forth
Persecution

The sermons in Part II are organized around sayings Jesus might have shared mostly with his disciples. In "Son of Man" he speaks about himself, who he is and why he has come. In "Brethren" he talks about discipleship. In "Going Forth" he tells disciples how to be teachers of the Word, and in "Persecution" he addresses the dangers disciples will face, especially after his death.

The enigmatic phrase *son of man* that Jesus often used to describe himself has always presented scholars and theologians with a conundrum because the Christian Church is founded on the assertion that Jesus was the only *son of God*. Yet Jesus himself apparently used that phrase rarely, and when he did it most often pointed to a state that anyone might attain to if they follow the Way, more like a synonym for entering Heaven.

The sayings of Jesus do not reveal a man who sought to become an object of worship based on his unique status, but rather one who offered himself as an example to be followed by those who want to become like him, who want to realize God as he does, who aspire to eternal Life.

An ancient Zen master once told his students, "I am just a finger pointing at the moon. Do not mistake the finger for the moon." The sayings of Jesus seem to tell us much the same thing.

6. Son of Man

God so loves the world that he reveals his One-begotten Son,   6.1
that whosoever becomes as him shall not perish,
but shall know eternal Life.

God sends the Son into the world not to condemn it,   6.2
but that through him the world might be saved.

The Son can do nothing of his own accord,   6.3
but only what he sees the Father doing.
For whatever the Father does, the Son does likewise.

The Father loves the Son, and shows him all   6.4
that he himself is doing. And greater works than these
will he show him, that you may marvel.
For as the Father raises the dead and gives them Life,
so also the Son gives Life to all whom he will.

I Am. And you will see the Son of Man, seated at   6.5
the right hand of Power, coming in the clouds of Heaven.

My teaching is not mine, but of the One who sends me.   6.6

He who sees me, sees the One who sends me.   6.7
He who receives me, receives the One who sends me.
I come as Light into the world,
that whoever receives me may not remain in darkness.

Whoever hears my Word but does not keep it,   6.8
I do not judge him. I come not to judge the world,
but to save the world.

You do not know what manner of spirit you are.   6.9
The Son of Man comes not to destroy lives, but to save them.

Those who are well have no need of a physician,   6.10
only those who are sick. I come not to call the righteous,
but the sinners to repentance. Go and learn what this means:
"I desire mercy, not sacrifice."

All things have been delivered to me by the Father.   6.11
No one knows the Son except the Father.
No one knows the Father except the Son,
and anyone to whom the Son wills to reveal him.

For it is the will of the Father that everyone   6.12
who knows the Son and receives him shall have eternal Life.
And I will raise him up at the last day.

He who keeps my Word and receives the Father who sends me,   6.13
finds eternal Life. He does not come into Judgment,
but passes from death to Life.

The Father judges no one, but gives all judgment to the Son,   6.14
that all may honor the Son, even as they honor the Father.
He who does not honor the Son
does not honor the Father who sends him.

For I have come from Heaven not to do my own will,   6.15
but the will of the One who sends me.
The will of the One who sends me is that I should lose nothing
of all that he has given me, but raise it up on the last day.

I can do nothing on my own authority. As I hear, I judge.   6.16
And my judgment is just, because I seek not my own will
but the will of the Father who sends me.

If anyone bears witness to himself, his testimony is not true.   6.17
Yet I bear witness to myself, and my testimony is true,
for I know whence I have come and whither I am going.
You do not know whence I come or whither I am going.

You judge according to the flesh. I judge no one.   6.18
Yet even if I do judge, my judgment is true,
for it is not I alone who judge,
but I and the One who sends me.

You search the scriptures because you think that in them   6.19
you will find eternal life.
It is these scriptures that bear witness to me,
yet you refuse to come to me that you may have Life!

You are from below. I am from above.   6.20
You are of this world. I am not of this world.

I bear witness to myself, just as the Father   6.21
who sends me bears witness to me.

I do not receive glory from men.   6.22
I know that you have not the love of God within you,
for I come in the name of God and you do not receive me.
Yet if another comes in his own name, him you would receive.

If I glorify myself, my glory is nothing.   6.23
It is the Father who glorifies me, he whom you say is your God.
But you do not know him. I know him.
If I said I do not know him, I would be a liar like you.
But I do know him, and I keep his Word.

If you knew God as your Father, you would love me,   6.24
for I proceed and come forth from God.
I come not of my own accord. God sends me.
Why do you not understand what I say?
It is because you cannot bear to hear my Word.

You do what you have heard from your earthly fathers.   6.25
I speak of what I have known with my Father in Heaven.

You ask that I tell you who I am so that you may believe in me?   6.26
You can read the face of the sky and of the earth,
but you do not know how to read this moment!
You do not recognize the One who is before you!

What if you saw the Son of Man returning   6.27
from whence he came?
It is the Spirit that gives Life. The flesh is of no avail.
The words I speak to you are Spirit and Life.
Yet there are some of you who do not believe.

Those I have chosen yet disbelieve me, for they are men.   6.28
I speak of what I know and bear witness to what I have seen.
But you do not believe my testimony.

If I tell you earthly things and you do not believe, 6.29
how can you believe when I tell you heavenly things?
No one enters into Heaven but he who comes from Heaven,
the Son of Man.

That flesh comes into being because of spirit is a wonder. 6.30
But if spirit came into being because of the flesh,
it would be a wonder of wonders.
Indeed, I am amazed at how the great wealth of spirit
has made its home in the great poverty of flesh.

I have not a demon. I honor the Father, yet you dishonor me. 6.31
I do not seek my own glory.
The One seeks it, and he will be the judge.
Whoever truly receives my Word will never know death.

You have received mercy. Do you not, then, desire to be filled? 6.32
Your heart is drunken. Do you not, then, desire to be sober?

Therefore be ashamed! Henceforth, waking or sleeping, 6.33
remember that you have seen the Son of Man,
and spoken with him in person, and listened to him in person.

You ask where is my Father? 6.34
You know neither me nor my Father.
If you knew me, you would know my Father also.

I have been with you so long, and still you do not know me? 6.35
How can you say, "Show us the Father"?
He who has seen me has seen the Father. Do you not know
that I am in the Father and the Father in me?

I do not speak these words on my own authority. 6.36
The Father who dwells in me does his works through me.
Believe me, I am in the Father and the Father in me.
Or else believe me because of the works themselves.

Truly, he who receives me will also do the works that I do. 6.37
And greater works than these will he do,
because I am in the Father.

Whatever you ask in my name, I will do it,   6.38
that the Father may be glorified in the Son.
If you ask anything in my name, I will do it.

I am the bread of Life. He who comes to me shall not hunger.   6.39
He who believes in me shall never thirst.

I am the living bread that comes from Heaven.   6.40
If anyone eats of this bread, he will know eternal Life.
This bread, which I give for the life of the world, is my flesh.

If anyone thirst, let him come to me and drink.   6.41
He who receives me, as the scripture has said,
"Out of his heart shall flow rivers of living water."

Everyone who drinks of earthly water will thirst again.   6.42
But whoever drinks of the water I shall give him
will never thirst. The water I shall give him will become in him
a spring of living water, welling up to eternal Life.

If you knew the gift of God, and who it is that is saying to you,   6.43
"Give me a drink," you would ask him for a drink,
and he would give you living water.

I am the resurrection and the Life.   6.44
He who receives me, though he die, yet shall he live.
Truly, whoever lives and becomes as me shall never die.
Do you believe this?

You and all who believe, and also those who yet will believe   6.45
in the One who sent me, I will cause to enter into Heaven,
to the place the Father has prepared for the elect and most elect.

And I will give to you the eternal morning star,   6.46
as I myself received it from the Father. And the Father
will give the rest he has promised, and eternal Life.

For the Son of Man has not come to be served, but to serve,   6.47
and to give his life as ransom for many. The Son of Man
has come to seek, and to save that which was lost.

As Moses lifted up the serpent in the wilderness,   6.48
so must the Son of Man be lifted up,
that whoever follows his Way shall have eternal Life.
For when I am lifted up, I will draw all men to myself.

And when you have lifted up the Son of Man,   6.49
you will know that I am he, and that I do nothing
on my own authority, but speak only as the Father taught me.
I have much to say about you and much to judge.

The One who sent me is true,   6.50
and I declare to the world what I have heard from him.
The One who sent me is with me. He has not left me alone,
and I always do what is pleasing to him.

Truly, the Spirit of God is upon me.   6.51
He has sent me to preach his Word to the poor in spirit.
He has sent me to heal the brokenhearted, declare liberty
to the captives and return sight to the blind.
He has sent me to set free the oppressed and proclaim
the glorious reign of the Lord.

As the lightning that flashes in one part of the heavens   6.52
lights also the other parts of the heavens,
so will it be with the Son of Man in his day.

You will see the heavens open, and the angels of God   6.53
ascending and descending upon the Son of Man.
But first he must suffer many things,
and be rejected by this generation.

Blessed are they who have known the Son before his coming,   6.54
that when I have come, I might return again.
Thrice blessed are they who were known by the Son before
they came to be, that you might have a place among them.

Everyone who has heard and learned from the Father   6.55
comes to me. Not that anyone has seen the Father,
except him who is from God. He has seen the Father.

No one can come to me unless the Father draws him 6.56
and brings him to me. And I will raise him up on the last day.
It is written in the prophets, "They shall all be taught by God."
Therefore, every man who has heard,
and has learned of the Father, comes unto me.

Heaven and earth will pass away, 6.57
but my Word will by no means pass away.

The time will come when you desire to live the days of 6.58
the Son of Man, but you will not be able to find him.
Others will tell you, "Look here!" or "Look there!"
Do not follow or go after them.

Foxes have their holes and birds have their nests, 6.59
but the Son of Man has nowhere to lay his head.

7. Brethren

I shall choose you,   7.1
one out of a thousand and two out of ten thousand,
and you shall stand as a single one.

You do not choose me. I choose you.   7.2
I appoint you, that you should go and bear fruit,
and that your fruit should abide, so that whatever
you ask the Father in my name, he may give it to you.

It is for your sakes I come. You are the beloved.   7.3
You are they who will be the cause of Life in many.
Invoke the Father, implore God often, and he will give to you.

Blessed is he who has seen the Son of Man   7.4
when he was proclaimed among the angels
and glorified among the saints. Yours is life.
Rejoice and be glad as sons of God.

Keep his will that you may be saved.   7.5
Accept reproof from me and save yourselves.
I intercede on your behalf with the Father,
and he will forgive you much.

We must do the work of him who sent me while it is day.   7.6
When darkness comes, no one can work.
As long as I am in the world, I am the Light of the world.

While you have the Light, receive the Light,   7.7
that you may become sons of Light.

Whoever believes in me and does the work of Light will live.   7.8
But whoever acknowledges what is light
yet does what is characteristic of darkness, has nothing
he can say in his defense, nor will he be able to raise his face
and look at the Son, who I am.

I will say to him, "You have sought and found,   7.9
you have asked and received. What do you blame me for?

Why did you withdraw from me and my kingdom?
You have acknowledged me and yet denied."
Now therefore, see that you are able to live as well as to die.

Do not make the kingdom of Heaven a desert within you.   7.10
Do not be proud because of the light that illumines,
but be to yourselves as I myself am to you.
It is for your sakes I have placed myself under the curse,
that you may be saved.

As long as I am with you, give heed to me and obey me.   7.11
When I depart from you, remember me. Remember me
because I was with you and you did not know me.
Blessed are they who know me.

Woe to those who have heard, yet do not believe.   7.12
Do you believe because you have seen me?
Blessed are they who have not seen me, yet believe.

Truly, blessed are they who do not see me and yet believe,   7.13
for they are called children of the Kingdom,
and are perfect in the perfect One.
To these I will become eternal Life in the kingdom of the Father.

You are my brothers and companions.   7.14
Our Father has delighted in you,
and in those who will believe in me through you.

Such great joy has our Father prepared for you that the angels   7.15
and the powers will desire to see it.
But they will not be allowed to see the greatness of our Father.

If you continue in my Word you are truly my disciples.   7.16
You will know Truth, and Truth will make you free.

Who is my mother and who are my brothers?   7.17
My mother and my brothers are those
who hear the word of God and do it.
My brethren are those who do the will of my Father.
It is they who will enter the kingdom of God.

Whoever does not disown his father and mother as I do,   7.18
cannot become a disciple to me.
And whoever does not embrace his true Father and true Mother
as I do, cannot become a disciple to me.

My mother birthed me into falsehood.   7.19
My true Mother gave me Life.

Truly, whoever comes to me and does not disown   7.20
his father and mother, wife and children, brothers and sisters,
and yes, his own life also, is not worthy of me.
If one does not disown his own soul he is not worthy of me.

Whoever desires to become as me, let him deny himself   7.21
and take up his cross in my Way. Let him follow me.

There is no one who has left house or brother or sister or   7.22
mother or father or children or land for my sake
and for the sake of Truth,
who will not receive a hundredfold, now in this time,
houses and brothers and sisters and mothers and fathers
and children and lands, and in the age to come, eternal Life.
For many who are last will be first, and the first last.

No one having put his hand to the plow,   7.23
who then looks back, is fit for the kingdom of God.

You know that the rulers of the Gentiles lord it over them,   7.24
and those who are called "benefactors"
exercise authority over them. But not so among you.

On the contrary, whoever desires to govern among you,   7.25
let him be your servant. And whoever desires to be first
among you, let him be the least —
just as the Son of Man did not come to be served, but to serve,
and to give his life as ransom for many.

You call me Teacher and Lord, and you are right, for so I am.   7.26
If I then, your lord and teacher, have washed your feet,
likewise you should wash one another's feet.

For I have given you an example,
that you should do for others as I have done for you.
If anyone would be first, he must be last of all,
and servant of all.

7.27

Who is considered greater — he who sits at the table
or he who serves? Is it not he who sits at the table?
Yet I am among you as one who serves.

7.28

A disciple is not above his teacher, nor a servant
above his master. It is enough for a disciple
to be like his teacher, and a servant to be like his master.

7.29

Truly, there are some of you who will not taste death
before you see the kingdom of God come with power.

7.30

8. The Female

He who is from Truth does not die.   8.1
He who is from the womb of woman, dies.

Death shall have power so long as women bear children.   8.2
I have come to undo the works of the womb.

When you see one who was not born of woman,   8.3
prostrate yourselves on your faces and worship him.
That one is your Father.

The head of the man is the Christ.   8.4
The head of the woman is the man.
Pray in the place where there is no man nor woman.

To you who say, "Let Mary leave us,   8.5
for women are not worthy of Life," I say that I myself
shall teach her as a male, so that she may become living Spirit.
For every female who becomes as a male
shall enter the kingdom of Heaven.

You ask why I love her more than all of you?   8.6
Ask rather why I do not love all of you as I do her.

Do you see this woman?   8.7
I entered your house and you gave me no water for my feet.
But she has washed my feet with her tears
and wiped them with the hair of her head.

You gave me no kiss, but this woman has not ceased   8.8
to kiss my feet since the time I came in.
You did not anoint my head with oil, but this woman
has anointed my feet with fragrant oil.

Leave her alone. Why do you trouble her?   8.9
She has done a beautiful thing for me.
For you shall have the poor with you always,
and whenever you will, you can do good to them.

But you will not always have me.   8.10
She has done what she could.
She has anointed my body beforehand for burying.
Truly, wherever the gospel is preached in the whole world,
what she has done will be told in memory of her.

Therefore I say to you, her sins, however many,   8.11
are forgiven, for she has loved much.
But to those who love little, little shall be forgiven.

Woman, your sins are forgiven.   8.12

9. Prayer

Let us go to the holy mountain and pray.   9.1

And when you pray, say something like this: 9.2
Our Father, who art in Heaven, hallowed be thy name.
Thy Kingdom come, thy will be done,
on earth as it is in Heaven. Give us this day our daily bread,
and forgive us our trespasses, as we forgive those
who trespass against us. And lead us not into temptation,
but deliver us from evil. For thine is the Kingdom,
and the power, and the glory, forever. Amen.

Hear us, Father, just as you have heard   9.3
your One-begotten Son, who you take to yourself
and give rest from many labors. Your power is great
and your weapons are mighty. You are the remembrance
and the serenity of the solitary ones.

Hear us, just as you have heard your elect,   9.4
who by your sacrifice enter in with their good deeds,
they who have redeemed their souls from these blind limbs
in order that they might know eternal Life.

I thank you, Father, lord of heaven and earth,   9.5
that you have hidden these things from the wise and prudent,
and revealed them to babes.
Even so, Father, for so it seemed good in your sight.

All things have been delivered to me by the Father.   9.6
No one knows the Son except the Father.
Nor does anyone know the Father except the Son,
and those whom the Son wills to reveal Him.

Therefore, I tell you, whatever you ask in prayer,   9.7
believe that you have received it, and it will be yours.

And whenever you stand praying,   9.8
forgive if you have anything against anyone,
so that your Father may also forgive you your trespasses.

In that day you will ask nothing of me.   9.9
But if you ask anything of the Father,
he will give it to you in my name.

Father, I thank you that you have heard me.   9.10
I know that you hear me always,
but I have said this on account of the people standing by,
that they may believe that I am from you.

I am good to you.   9.11
Alleluia.
I am meek and kind to you.
Alleluia.
Glory be to you, O Lord, for I give myself to all who desire me.
Alleluia.
Glory be to you, O Lord, world without end. Amen.
Alleluia.

10. Going Forth

Peace to you. My peace I give to you.   10.1

You are the salt of the earth. Salt is good.   10.2
But if salt loses its savor, how can salt be seasoned?
It is good for nothing, fit neither for the fields nor the dunghill,
but is thrown out to be trampled underfoot by beasts and men.
Have salt in yourselves. Be at peace with one another.

Let the dead bury their dead. Become passers-by.   10.3
Go and proclaim the kingdom of God. Go into all the world
and teach the gospel of Truth to the whole of Creation.

For the hearts of the people have grown dull.   10.4
Their ears are hard of hearing and their eyes have closed,
lest they should see with their eyes and hear with their ears,
lest they should understand with their hearts
and turn around, so that I might heal them.

Blessed are your eyes, for they see, and your ears, for they hear.   10.5
Truly I say to you, many prophets and righteous men
have desired to see what you see, yet did not see it,
to hear what you hear, yet did not hear it.

Go and teach disciples in all nations,   10.6
baptizing them in the name of the Father, and of the Son,
and of the Holy Spirit. Teach them to observe all
that I have given you. And remember,
I am with you always, even to the end of the age.

If they ask, "Where did you come from?" say to them,   10.7
"We come from the Light, the place where the Light
comes into being of its own accord and establishes itself,
and becomes manifest through these images."

If they ask, "Are you the Light?" say to them,   10.8
"We are its children, the elect of the living Father."
And if they ask, "What is the sign of the Father in you?"
tell them, "It is movement and stillness."

You may entrust these mysteries to all who are faithful   10.9
and can keep them for themselves.
For there are some who are worthy of them.

But there are others to whom these mysteries   10.10
ought not be entrusted — boasters, drunkards, idolaters,
seducers, slanderers, teachers of falsehood, the proud,
the merciless, and doers of all the works of the devil —
such as these are not worthy to be entrusted with them.

Do not give what is holy to dogs, lest they turn it to dung.   10.11
Do not cast your pearls before swine, lest they trample them,
then turn on you and tear you to pieces.

These mysteries shall be kept secret   10.12
from those who cannot contain them.
But all who can contain them shall have a share in them.

You are blessed, my beloved, and all who are like you   10.13
are blessed in having this message entrusted to them.
For all who truly understand it shall receive all they wish
in all times of my Judgment.

You are the light of the world.   10.14
One does not light a candle and put it under a basket,
but sets it on a lampstand so that it may give light
to all in the house.

Let your light so shine before men, that they may see   10.15
your good works and glorify your Father in Heaven.
A city set high on a mountain cannot be hidden, nor can it fall.

What I tell you in the dark, speak in the light.   10.16
What I whisper in your ear, preach from the housetops.
Nothing is hidden, except to be made manifest.
Nothing is secret, except that it come into light.

Go your way. I send you out as lambs among wolves.   10.17
Heal the sick, cleanse the lepers, cast out demons,
raise the dead. Freely you have received, freely give.

Take nothing for the journey, neither staff, nor bag,   10.1?
nor bread, nor spare sandals, nor two tunics.
Carry neither gold nor silver nor copper in your money belts,
for a worker is worthy of his food. Greet no one along the road.

Whatever city or town you enter, inquire who in it is worthy   10.1?
and stay there until you leave. Whatever house you enter, say,
"Peace to this house." And if a son of peace is there,
your peace will rest upon it. If not, it will return to you.

Whoever will not receive you nor hear your words,   10.2?
when you depart from that house or city, shake off
the very dust from your feet as a testimony against them.
Truly, in the day of Judgment it will be more tolerable
for the land of Sodom and Gomorrah than for that city.

When you go into any land, walk about the districts.   10.21
If they receive you, heal the sick among them
and eat whatever food they set before you.

If you fast, you will give rise to sin for yourselves.   10.22
If you pray, you will be condemned.
If you give alms, you will do harm to your spirits.

What goes into your mouth will not defile you.   10.23?
It is what issues from your mouth that will defile you.
What goes into a man from outside cannot defile him,
since it enters not his heart but his stomach, and so passes on.

It is from within, out of the heart of a man, that issues murder,   10.24
theft, adultery, coveting, wickedness, deceit, licentiousness,
envy, slander, pride, evil thoughts, blasphemy and foolishness.
All these evil things come from within.
These are the things that defile a man.
To eat with unwashed hands does not defile a man.

Go then and preach. Be good ministers and servants.   10.25
Preach concerning the coming, and the mercy of the Father.

Preach and teach, and I will be with you.
And I am well pleased to be with you, that you may become
joint heirs with me to the Kingdom of him whom I am from.

10.26

Preach and teach truly and rightly, respecting and fearing
the person of no one, neither rich nor poor,
but especially not that of the rich, among whom are found
those who revel in their riches and do not follow my Way.
Yet as soon as any of these gives, and does not deny to him
who has nothing, he shall be called a disciple.

10.27

Do not go into the land of the Gentiles, nor enter a city
of the Samaritans. Go to the lost sheep of Israel and teach,
saying, "The kingdom of Heaven is before you."

10.28

Preach to the twelve tribes of Israel, to the Gentiles of Israel,
and to the land of Israel to the east and west, north and south,
that many will come to know the Son of Man.

10.29

Do not be called "rabbi,"
for the One is your rabbi, the Christ,
and you are all brethren.
Do not be called "teacher,"
for the One is your teacher, the Christ,
and you are all brethren.

10.30

And do not call anyone on earth "father,"
for the One is your Father, he who abides in Heaven.
He who is the greatest among you shall be your servant.

10.31

He who receives you receives me,
and he who receives me receives Him who sent me.
He who receives a prophet in the name of a prophet
shall receive a prophet's reward.
He who receives a righteous man in the name of
a righteous man shall receive a righteous man's reward.

10.32

And whoever gives even one of these little ones
only a cup of cold water in the name of a disciple,
assuredly, he shall by no means lose his reward.

10.33

If you see a man casting out demons in my name,   10.34
do not forbid him, even though he is not following us.
For no one who does a mighty work in my name
will be able soon after to speak evil of me.

He that is not against us, is for us. Truly, whoever gives you   10.35
a cup of water to drink because you proclaim the Christ,
will by no means lose his reward.

As my Father has done through me, I will also do through you,   10.36
for I am with you, and I give you my peace and my spirit
and my power, that others may know Truth. This power
I will also give to them, that they may give it to the Gentiles.

I have spoken it to you and you have understood.   10.37
Go forth now and preach, guided by the hand of the Son,
who is perfect, that his work may be sanctified.
You are chosen in the hope that I have given you.

Spread my gospel throughout the whole world in peace!   10.38
There will be rejoicing at the source of my Word,
the hope of Life, and the world will be suddenly carried off.

You will become fathers and teachers and servants.   10.39
All who listen to you and believe in my Way will receive
the light of the seal that is in my hand, and through me
you will become fathers and teachers.

They will call you fathers, for you, full of love and compassion,   10.40
revealed to them what is in Heaven, and by my hand
they will receive forgiveness and the baptism of life.

They will call you teachers, for you delivered to them my Word,   10.41
and warned them, and they turned back in the things for which
you rebuked them. You were not afraid of their riches
and did not respect their persons.

You kept the Word of the Father and did it. You have a reward   10.42
with the Father in Heaven. You have forgiveness of sins,
and eternal Life, and a share of the Kingdom.

Do not be grieved. You are my brothers,
companions in the kingdom of Heaven with our Father,
for so has it pleased him. Also to those you teach, and who
become followers of my Word, I give this hope.

10.43

Peace be with you. Receive my peace to yourselves.
Beware that no one lead you astray, saying, "Lo here!"
or "Lo there!" The Son of Man is within you,
and those who seek him will find him. Find him!

10.44

Go then and preach the gospel of the Kingdom.
Do not lay down any rules beyond what I appointed for you.
Do not give a law like the lawgivers,
lest you be constrained by it.

10.45

As the Father has sent me, so I send you.
Receive the Holy Spirit.
If you forgive the sins of any, they are forgiven.
If you retain the sins of any, they are retained.

10.46

I give you the authority to trample on serpents and scorpions,
and over all the power of the enemy,
and nothing shall by any means hurt you.

10.47

Nevertheless do not rejoice in this,
that the spirits are subject to you, but rather rejoice because
your names are written in Heaven.

10.48

Love one another and honor each other,
that continual peace may reign among you.
What you do not want done to you,
that do to no one else. Love your enemies.

10.49

Teach this to those who believe in me,
and preach concerning the kingdom of the Father.
As my Father has given me the power, so I give it to you,
that you may bring near the children of the Father.

10.50

Preach, and they will believe. You are the one
whose duty it is to lead His children into Heaven.

10.51

11. Persecution

A prophet is not without honor   11.1
except in his own country and his own house.

No prophet is accepted in his own village.   11.2
No healer can heal those who know him.

If the world hates you, know that the world hated me   11.3
before it hated you. If you were of the world,
the world would love its own. But you are not of the world.
I chose you out of the world, therefore the world hates you.

Remember what I told you: 11.4
"A servant is not greater than his master."
Those who have kept my Word will keep yours also.
Those who have persecuted me will also persecute you.

They will do this to you on my account because   11.5
they do not know him who sent me. If I had not come
and spoken to them, they would not know they have sin.
But now they know, and have no excuse for their sin.

If I had not done among them the works that no one else did,   11.6
they would not have sin. But now they have seen and hated
both me and my Father. It is to fulfill the word that is written
in their law, "They hated me without a cause."

You will be hated by all because of me, but he who endures   11.7
to the end will be saved. When they persecute you in one city,
flee to another. Truly, you will not have gone through
the cities of Israel before the Son of Man comes.

They will deliver you up to be afflicted and kill you.   11.8
Many of you will be offended, and hate one another,
and betray one another. You will be betrayed
even by parents and brothers, relatives and friends.
And you will be hated by all nations because of me.

Some of you they will put to death. Yet not a hair of   11.9
your head shall be lost. By your patience possess your soul.

You will be sheep among wolves.   11.10
Therefore be wise as serpents and harmless as doves.
But let the sheep not fear the wolves after death.

Fear not them who can kill you but otherwise   11.11
cannot do anything to you. Fear Him who after your death
has power over body and soul.

Truly, do not fear those who can kill the body but afterwards   11.12
can do no more. I will tell you whom you should fear,
fear Him who, after he has killed, has the power
to cast you into Hell. Fear Him!

Are not two sparrows sold for a copper coin? And not one   11.13
of them falls to the ground apart from your Father's will.
The very hairs of your head are all numbered.
Do not fear. You are of more value than many sparrows.

Whoever confesses me before men, him also   11.14
will the Son of Man confess before our Father in Heaven.
But whoever denies me before men,
will be denied before our Father in Heaven.

Take heed for yourselves. For before all these things   11.15
they will beat you, and persecute you, and deliver you up
to synagogues and councils, and scourge you in their prisons.
You will be brought before governors and kings because of me
and forced to answer and give testimony to them.

On these occasions speak first the gospel of Truth,   11.16
for in this way it will spread to all nations.
Remember your first duty. Proclaim the gospel of Truth to all.

Do not concern yourself with what you should say.   11.17
I will give you a mouth. I will give you words
that no adversary can refute or contradict.

So when they take you to the magistrates and authorities,   11.18
do not worry about how or what you should answer.
The Holy Spirit will teach you in that very hour what to say.
It is not you who speaks. It is the Holy Spirit.

Anyone who speaks against the Son of Man,   11.19
it will be forgiven him. But whoever speaks against
the Holy Spirit, it will not be forgiven him,
either in this age or in the age to come.
Truly, every other sin and blasphemy will be forgiven,
but blasphemy against the Holy Spirit will not be forgiven.

Either the tree is good and its fruit is good, or the tree is bad   11.20
and its fruit is bad. A tree is known by its fruit.

Those who desire to see the face of God,   11.21
who do not regard the person of the sinful rich,
who do not fear men who lead them astray, but reprove them —
they will be crowned in the presence of the Father.
Those who reprove their neighbors will also be saved.
These are the sons of wisdom and faith.

If someone does not become a son of wisdom and faith,   11.22
he will hate and persecute, and not turn towards his brother,
but will despise him and cast him away.

But those who walk in Truth, and in the knowledge of faith   11.23
in me, and in the knowledge of wisdom, and who persevere
for righteousness — regardless that men despise those who
strive against poverty and endure — great is their reward.

Those who are reviled and tormented and persecuted   11.24
because they are destitute and men are arrogant
against them, who hunger and thirst yet persevere —
blessed will they be in Heaven. And they will be there
with me always. But woe to those who hate and despise them!
Their end is for destruction.

I tell you these things so that you might remain steadfast.   11.25
They will throw you out of the synagogues and worse.
Indeed, the hour is coming when those who kill you
will believe they are serving God. They will do this because
they do not know God, nor me.

Chapter III
Wandering Prophet

Ignorance and Sin
The Ten Commandments
Faith and Miracles
Law and Scriptures
False Prophets
Miscellany

It is said that Jesus' ministry lasted one to three years, during which time he traveled from place to place, teaching wherever people would listen, healing whenever they asked. The sermons in Part III tend to include sayings and teachings Jesus might have spoken to general listeners in public, as well as to his closer disciples.

We hear Jesus admonishing the "ignorant" for ignoring their existential dilemma of being, as W.B. Yeats puts it, "fastened to a dying animal," and warning of dire consequences if they do not repent of their ignorance and seek a way out. We see him healing the sick and preaching to them that it is their belief that heals them, not his powers.

We also see him as a student of scripture, well versed in what is now called the Old Testament, and often referring to it for support and examples. Though his own teachings were revolutionary, Jesus did not reject most of the existing scriptures, but rather, expounded and expanded on them. What we do hear him reject, vehemently, is the hypocrisy and spiritual crimes of religious authorities, and the false prophets who turn the heads of the ignorant to their purposes.

The "Miscellany" sermon contains all the sayings of Jesus that did not find a home in other *Christ Sutras* sermons, and thus does not flow like the others.

12. Ignorance and Sin

It is necessary I speak to you of certain things,   12.1
because this is the teaching for the perfect.
If you desire to become perfect, you must observe these things.
If not, you shall remain ignorant.

It is impossible for a wise man to dwell with a fool.   12.2
For the wise man is perfect in all wisdom,
while the fool cannot even discern between good and bad.
The wise man is nourished by Truth,
like a tree growing by a meandering stream.

The ignorant, although they have wings, are attracted   12.3
to the visible forms, things that are far from Truth.
For that which drives them, the fire,
gives them an illusion of truth.

It shines on them with perishable beauty,   12.4
imprisons them in dark sweetness,
and captivates them with fragrant pleasure.

It blinds them with insatiable lust and burns their souls.   12.5
It becomes for them a stake in the heart
they can never dislodge. And like a bit in the mouth,
it leads them according to its own desire.

It fetters them with chains and binds   12.6
all their limbs with the bitter bond of lust for visible things,
things that decay, and change, and swerve by impulse.

The ignorant are always attracted downwards.   12.7
And as they are killed they are assimilated into the substance
of all beasts, the substance of the perishable realm.

Therefore, it is useful for you to be among your own.   12.8
It is good for you because things visible among men
will dissolve, for the vessel of their flesh will dissolve.
And when it is brought to naught, it will become again
among the visible things, the things that are seen.

That which is visible dissolves soon after it becomes visible.   12.9
Then shapeless shadows emerge, and in the midst of tombs,
the ignorant dwell upon corpses, in pain and corruption of soul.

And the fire burns them with pain and regret   12.10
on account of their yearning for the faith they have lost.
And they are gathered back to that which is visible.

Even those who see that which is not visible,   12.11
yet have not the first love, will perish in the concern for this life,
and the scorching of the fire.

Woe to you, godless ones, who have no hope,   12.12
who rely on things that will not happen!
Woe to you who hope in the flesh
and in the prison that will perish!

Do you think the imperishable will also perish?   12.13
How long will you be oblivious?
Your belief is set upon the world and your god is this life!
You are corrupting your soul!

Woe to you, for the fire that burns in you is insatiable!   12.14
Woe to you because of the wheel that turns in your minds!

Woe to you because of the burning that is in you.   12.15
For it will devour your flesh openly, rend your souls secretly,
and prepare you for your companions!

Woe to you, captives, for you are bound in caverns!   12.16
You laugh! In mad laughter you rejoice!
You neither realize your perdition, nor do you reflect
on your circumstances, nor have you understood
that you dwell in darkness and death!

On the contrary, you are drunk with the fire of desire   12.17
and full of bitterness. Your mind is deranged
because of the burning that is in you, and sweet to you
is the crown of your enemies' blows!

The darkness rose for you like the light,
and you surrendered your freedom for servitude!
You darkened your hearts and surrendered
your thoughts to folly. You filled your mind
with the smoke of the fire that is in you!

Your light is hidden in the cloud of darkness.
You were deceived into pursuing the garment put upon you.
You were seized by belief in the false.

And who is it you have believed? Do you not understand
that you dwell among those who want you to curse yourself
as if your promise were nonexistent?
You baptized your soul in the water of darkness!
You walked by your own whims!

Satan makes war against you and veils your understanding.
The offerings of this world conquer you. Your eyes
must be opened and your ears unstopped, so that you may
enter the tabernacle not made by the hand of man, but which
our Father in Heaven has made for me and for the elect.

Get behind me, Satan! You are an offense to me.
For you are not mindful of the things of God,
but of the things of men.

Woe to the world because of offenses!
It is impossible that no offenses should come,
but woe to him through whom they do come!

If your right hand causes you to sin, cut it off and cast it
from you. It is better for you that one of your members perish,
than for your whole body to be thrown into Hell.

If your right eye causes you to sin, pluck it out and cast it
from you. It is better for you to enter the kingdom of God
with one eye, than with two eyes be thrown into Hell,
where the worm does not die, and the fire is not quenched,
and everyone is salted with fire.

Until you are transformed and become as little children,   12.26
you will by no means enter the kingdom of Heaven.
For whoever humbles himself as a little child
is the greatest in the kingdom of Heaven.

And whoever receives one little child like this in my name,   12.27
receives me. But whoever should despise
one of these little ones, or cause a child to sin,
it would be better for him if a great millstone were hung
around his neck and he were drowned in the depth of the sea.

Take heed, therefore, that you do not offend the little ones.   12.28
I say to you that in Heaven their angels
gaze eternally upon the face of the Father.
For the Son of Man has come to save that which was lost.

He who sins is the slave of sin. A slave does not continue   12.29
in the house forever. The Son continues forever.
So if you are made free through the Son, you are free indeed.

Watch and pray that you may not enter into temptation.   12.30
The spirit is willing, but the flesh is weak.

Woe to you who love immorality and intimacy of the flesh!   12.31
Woe to you because of the powers of the body that afflict you!
Woe to you because of the forces of the evil demons!
Woe to you who beguile your limbs with the fire!

Who will shower refreshing rain upon you   12.32
to extinguish the molten fire of your burning?
Who will cause the sun to shine upon you,
to dispel your inner darkness and drain the polluted water?

Woe to the souls that spurn their own judgment!   12.33
I see men delight their souls in vanity
and abandon themselves to the unclean world.
I see how all of it is for the benefit of the enemy!

Therefore I stand by them and say, "O you souls that   12.34
apply yourself to uncleanliness and have no fear before God!"

Woe to you who lack an advocate!   12.35
Woe to you who stand in need of grace!
Blessed are they who speak out and obtain grace for themselves.

You are like a foreigner. How are foreigners seen in the eyes   12.36
of your city? Why do you complain when you have cast
yourselves away of your own accord and separated yourself
from your home? Why have you abandoned your home
of your own accord, and made it ready for those
who want to dwell in it? O you outcasts and fugitives!
Woe to you, for you will be caught!

Or do you perhaps think that the Father is a lover of mankind,   12.37
or that he is won over without prayers,
or that he grants remission to one on another's behalf,
or that he bears with one who asks?
He knows your desire. He knows what the flesh needs!

Or do you think it is not this flesh that desires the soul?   12.38
Without the soul the body does not sin,
just as the soul is not saved without the spirit.

If the soul is saved when it is without evil, and the spirit   12.39
is also saved, then the body becomes free from sin.

The spirit quickens the soul, but the body kills it.   12.40
It is the soul that kills itself. Truly, he will not by any means
forgive the soul the sin, nor the flesh the guilt.

None of those who have worn the flesh will be saved.   12.41
Do you think that many have found the kingdom of Heaven?
Blessed is he who is even the fourth one to find Heaven!

Woe to you for whose sakes I was sent to this place.   12.42
Once more I reprove you, you who are.
Become like those who are not,
that you may be with those who are not.
Blessed are they who enter the Father.

And woe to you who do not accept that you are teachers.   12.43
Now the ignorant labor at preaching instead of you,
while you rush into recklessness.

Understand that some of you have been sent to rescue   12.44
those the ignorant kill daily, that they might arise from death.

13. The Ten Commandments

Why do you call me good?   13.1
No one is good but the One, that is, God.

If you want to enter into Life, keep the commandments.   13.2
You know the commandments:
Do not murder. Do not commit adultery. Do not steal.
Do not bear false witness. Honor your father and your mother.

You have heard it was said to those of old,   13.3
"You shall not murder, and whoever murders
shall be in danger of the Judgment."

I say to you that whoever is angry with his brother   13.4
without a cause shall also be in danger of the Judgment.
And whoever says to his brother, "Raca!" shall be in danger
of the council. And whoever says, "You fool!"
shall be in danger of Hell fire.

You have heard it was said, "You shall not commit adultery."   13.5
I say to you that whoever looks at a woman with lust
has already committed adultery with her in his heart.

You have heard it was said, "Whoever divorces his wife,   13.6
let him give her a certificate of divorce."
I say to you that whoever divorces his wife for any reason
except infidelity causes her to commit adultery.

And whoever divorces his wife and marries another,   13.7
commits adultery against her. And if a woman divorces
her husband and marries another, she commits adultery.
And whoever marries a divorced woman commits adultery.

It is because of your hardness of heart that he gave you   13.8
this commandment. Have you not read that in the beginning
of Creation, "God made them male and female.
For this reason a man shall leave his father and mother
and be joined to his wife, and the two shall become one flesh"?

So then, they are no longer two, but one flesh,   13.9
and what God has joined together, let not man separate.

There is no sin, but it is you who create sin   13.10
when you do things like adultery, which are called "sin."
That is why the Good came into your midst,
to the essence of every nature, in order to restore it to its root.

Therefore, he who is married should not divorce his wife.   13.11
But he who is not married should not marry.
The unmarried should think day and night on godly things.

The sons of this age marry and are given in marriage.   13.12
But those who are counted worthy to attain the age to come
and the resurrection from the dead,
neither marry nor are given in marriage.

Nor can they anymore die, being sons of the resurrection.   13.13
For they are equal to the angels of Heaven,
and are sons of God.

You have heard it was said, "You shall not swear falsely,   13.14
but shall perform your oaths to the Lord."
I say to you, do not swear at all.
Neither by Heaven, for it is God's throne,
nor by the earth, for it is God's footstool,
nor by Jerusalem, for it is the city of the great king.

Nor shall you swear by your head,   13.15
because you cannot make one hair white or black.
Just let your "Yes" mean yes, and your "No" mean no.
For whatever is more than this is from the evil one.

You have heard it was said, "An eye for an eye   13.16
and a tooth for a tooth." But I say to you, resist not evil.

Whoever strikes you on your right cheek, turn the other to him.   13.17
Whoever takes your coat, let him also have your shirt.
Whoever compels you to go one mile,
go for two miles with him. Give to him who asks,
and from him who wants to borrow, do not turn away.

You have heard it was said, "Love your neighbor
and hate your enemy." I say to you, love your enemies.

Bless those who curse you. Do good to those who hate you.
Pray for those who spitefully use and persecute you,
that you may be sons of our Father in Heaven.

For God makes his sun rise on both the evil and the good,
and sends his rain upon the just and unjust alike.

Truly, keep all these commandments, yet even as you do
you will still lack one thing. If you want to be perfect,
go sell what you have and give to the poor.
You will have treasure in Heaven.

14. Faith and Miracles

Things that are impossible with men 14.1
are possible with God. Have faith in God.

If two on earth agree concerning anything that they ask, 14.2
it will be done for them by the Father.
Truly, if two become one in this house, they can say
to the mountain, "Move away," and it will move away.

For where two or more are gathered together in my name, 14.3
I am there in the midst of them.

Until now, you have asked nothing in the name of Christ. 14.4
Ask and you will receive, that your joy may be full.
Whatever you ask in prayer, believing, you will receive.

Truly, if you have but faith the size of a mustard seed, 14.5
you can say to this mulberry tree, "Be pulled up by the roots
and be planted in the sea," and it would obey you.

If you have but faith as a mustard seed, 14.6
you can say to this mountain, "Move from here to there,"
and it will move. Nothing will be impossible for you.

Believe me, whoever says to this mountain, 14.7
"Be taken up and cast into the sea," and does not doubt
in his heart, but believes that what he says will come to pass,
it will be done for him.

If you can, believe! Do not fear, only believe. 14.8
All things are possible for him who believes.

Did I not tell you that if you would believe 14.9
you would know the glory of God?
Yet unless you see signs and wonders you do not believe.

"Lord, I am not worthy that you should enter my house, 14.10
but only speak your word and my servant shall be healed."
I marvel at your words, Centurion.

Truly, I have not found such great faith, no, not in Israel!   14.11
Many will come from east and west and sit down with
Abraham, Isaac and Jacob in the kingdom of Heaven.
But the sons of the kingdom of earth will be cast into
outer darkness. There will be weeping and gnashing of teeth.

Go your way, Centurion. As you believe, let it be done for you.   14.12
Your servant shall be healed this same hour.

If anyone comes in faith to be healed, I ask them only,   14.13
"Do you believe I am able to do this?"
For according to your faith it shall be for you.
I will come and heal you.
And when you are healed, see that you tell no one.

To this paralytic on a pallet I say,   14.14
"Be of good cheer. Your sins are forgiven you."

Do you think I blaspheme? Why do you doubt in your heart?   14.15
Which is easier, to say "Arise and walk,"
or to have the power to forgive sins?

But so you may know that the Son of Man has the power   14.16
to forgive sins, I say also to this man,
"Arise, take up your pallet and walk to your house."

To this leper who asks to be cleansed I say,   14.17
"I am willing. You are cleansed. But see that you tell no one.
Go your way, show yourself to the priests and offer the gift
that Moses commanded as a testimony to them."

To this blind man I say, "Your sight is now restored.   14.18
Sin no more, that nothing worse befall you.
Your faith has saved you. Go in peace."

To this mother I say, "O woman, great is your faith!   14.19
Let it be as you desire. Your daughter is not dead
but is healed this very hour."

To this young woman I say, "Arise. Be of good cheer.   14.20
Your faith has made you well."

And now I have compassion for the multitude.   14.21
They have continued with me three days and have nothing
to eat. I do not want to send them away hungry,
lest they faint on the way. Give them something to eat.

Why do you reason among yourselves because you have   14.22
brought no bread? Do you not yet understand?
Do you not remember the five loaves into five thousand
and how many baskets you took up? Or the seven loaves
into four thousand and how many baskets you took up?

It is written, "Man shall not live by bread alone,   14.23
but by every word that proceeds from the mouth of God."

O ye of little faith, why do you doubt? Where is your faith?   14.24

Why are you afraid? Have you no faith?   14.25
Behold, I rebuke the winds and sea, and there is great calm.
With faith, you shall do likewise.

By what authority do I do these things?   14.26
I will ask you one question, and if you can answer,
then I will tell you by what authority I do these things.
The baptism of John whence was it? From Heaven, or men?
If you cannot tell me, then neither will I tell you
by what authority I do these things.

Go and tell John the things you witness.   14.27
The blind see and the lame walk. The lepers are cleansed
and the deaf hear. The dead are raised up
and the poor have the gospel preached to them.

Blessed is he who is not offended because of me.   14.28

15. Law and Scriptures

Do not think I come to destroy the law or the prophets.   15.1
I do not come to destroy, but to fulfill.

Truly, until heaven and earth pass away, not one jot   15.2
nor one tittle will pass from the law until all is fulfilled.

You err because you do not know the true things   15.3
of the scriptures. And because of this,
you also know nothing of the power of God.
Why do you not understand what is plain in the scriptures?

Adam came into being from a great power and a great wealth,   15.4
but he did not become worthy.
Had he been worthy, he would not have experienced death.

It was not Moses who gave you bread from Heaven.   15.5
The Father gives you the true bread from Heaven.
For the bread of God is that which comes from Heaven
and gives life to the world.

How can you believe those who receive glory only from   15.6
one another, yet do not seek the glory that comes from God?

Do not think that I shall accuse you to the Father.   15.7
It is Moses who accuses you, on whom you set your hope.
If you believed Moses you would believe me,
for he wrote of me. But if you do not believe his writings,
how will you believe my words?

As for the dead being raised, have you not read   15.8
in the book of Moses, in the passage about the bush,
what God said to him? "I am the God of Abraham,
the God of Isaac, and the God of Jacob."
God is the God of the living, not the dead. For all live in Him.

I heal one man on the Sabbath and you say that the law   15.9
has been broken. Moses gave you circumcision—
not that it is from Moses, but from the fathers—
so you circumcise a man on the Sabbath.

If on the Sabbath a man receives circumcision so that   15.10
the law of Moses is not broken, are you angry with me
because on the Sabbath I made a man's whole body well?

If circumcision were beneficial, fathers would beget sons   15.11
already circumcised from their mother.
Yet, the true circumcision in spirit is of priceless value.

The Sabbath was made for man, not man for the Sabbath.   15.12
The Son of Man is lord even of the Sabbath.

Which of you, having a donkey or an ox that has fallen   15.13
into a pit, will not immediately pull him out,
though it be on the Sabbath day?

Have you not read what David did when he was hungry,   15.14
he and those who were with him? How he entered the house
of God and ate the showbread, which was not lawful for him to
eat, nor for those who were with him, but only for the priests?
Have you not read in the law that on the Sabbath the priests
in the temple profane the Sabbath and are blameless?

In this place there is One greater than the temple.   15.15

Pharisees, what do you think of Christ? Whose son is he?   15.16
How can you say Christ is the son of David?
How then does David in spirit call him "Lord"?

David himself says in the Book of Psalms: 15.17
"The Lord said to my Lord, sit at my right hand
until I make your enemies your footstool."
If David calls the Christ "Lord," how is he then his son?

You say, "Twenty-four prophets spoke in Israel   15.18
and all of them spoke in you." Yet you have omitted the one
living in your presence and have spoken only of the dead.

You inquire how to prophesy and become an oracle? Do you
not know that the head of prophecy was cut off with John?

15.19

The law and the prophets were until John.
Since that time the kingdom of God has been preached,
and everyone is pressing into it.

15.20

What did you go out into the wilderness to see?
A reed shaken by the wind? A man clothed in soft garments
like your kings and your great men?
They wear fine garments but are unable to discern the truth.

15.21

What did you go out to see? A prophet?
Yes, I say to you, and more than a prophet. For this is he
of whom it is written: "Behold, I send my messenger
before you, and he will prepare the way for you."

15.22

Among those born of women there is no greater prophet
than John the Baptist. Yet he who is least
in the kingdom of God is far greater than he.
Truly, whoever among you becomes as a little child
will enter the Kingdom and be superior to John.

15.23

The testimony I receive is not from man, but I say this
that you may be saved. John was a burning and shining lamp,
and you were willing to rejoice for awhile in his light.

15.24

The testimony I have is far greater than that of John.
For the works the Father has granted me to accomplish—
these very works which I am doing—
bear witness that I am from the Father.

15.25

John neither eats nor drinks so priests say, "He has a demon."
The Son of Man eats and drinks so they say, "Look, a glutton
and a drunk, a friend of tax collectors and sinners!"
But wisdom is justified by her children.

15.26

The scribes and Pharisees have taken the keys of Knowledge
and hidden them. They themselves have not entered,
nor have they allowed to enter those who wish to.
Therefore, be as wise as serpents and as innocent as doves.

15.27

The scribes and the Pharisees sit in Moses' seat.　15.28
Therefore whatever they tell you to observe and do,
that observe and do. But do not do according to their works.
For they say, yet do not do. They bind heavy burdens,
hard to bear, and lay them on men's shoulders,
but they themselves lift not one finger to remove them.

Truly, unless your righteousness exceeds the righteousness　15.29
of the scribes and Pharisees, you will by no means
enter the kingdom of Heaven.

From whom do the kings of the earth take customs and taxes,　15.30
from their sons or from strangers?
From strangers, surely, for then their sons are free.

Nevertheless, lest we offend them, go to the sea,　15.31
cast in a hook, and take the fish that comes up first.
Open its mouth and you will find a piece of money.
Take that and give it to them for me and you.

Be good money changers. Render unto Caesar the things　15.32
that are Caesar's, and to God the things that are God's.

And if you bring your gift to the altar, and there remember　15.33
that your brother has something against you, leave your gift
there before the altar, and go your way. First be reconciled
to your brother, then come and offer your gift.

And when you go with your adversary to the magistrate,　15.34
make every effort along the way to settle with him,
lest he drag you to the judge, and the judge deliver you
to the officer, and the officer throw you into prison.
I tell you, you shall not depart from there
until you have paid the last penny.

Be a friend to those of unrighteous mammon, that when　15.35
your body fails, you may be received into an eternal home.
For he who is faithful in what is least, is faithful also in much.
And he who is unjust in what is least, is unjust also in much.

For if you have not been faithful in unrighteous mammon,   15.36
who will commit to your trust true riches?
If you have not been faithful in what is another's,
who will give you what is your own?

The angels and prophets will come and give you   15.37
the things that are already yours. And you will give them
the things that you have, and you will say to yourselves,
"When will they come and take what is theirs?"

You have learned from the scriptures that the prophets   15.38
spoke of my coming. Their prophecy has been fulfilled in me,
and now you must become a leader for them.

You will meet a man named Saul, which is translated as Paul.   15.39
He is a Jew, circumcised in accordance with the law.
And he will hear my voice from the heavens,
and it will fill him with fear and trembling.
His eyes will be dark and his face will be laced with spittle.

Everything I have spoken to you and everything   15.40
you have written about me you must deliver to Paul.
Remind him that I fulfill the scriptures and deliver him
to my Word. He will work for the salvation of the Gentiles.

Give to him what I have given you. Teach him my Way.   15.41
Tell him I am in God and God is in me. Immediately his eyes
will be opened, and he will praise God in Heaven.

And he will become strong among the nations,   15.42
and he will preach and teach, and many will be delighted
when they hear him, and many will be saved.

Then he will be hated. He will be delivered into the hands   15.43
of his enemy and brought up to testify before their king.
And the king shall hear his complete testimony of me.

And though the king persecuted me and hated me,   15.44
he will repent and be converted to my Way. And the king
will preach and teach my Word, and he will become an elect,
a chosen vessel, a wall that does not fall.

So shall it be that the last of the last shall become a preacher   15.45
to the Gentiles, perfect to the will of the Father.

On these accounts I descended, and have spoken   15.46
with your fathers, the prophets, Abraham, Isaac and Jacob,
and have brought them the news that you may be received
from the realm below into Heaven.

And I have given you the right hand of the baptism of Life,   15.47
and forgiveness and pardon for all wickedness as to you,
and from now on also, forgiveness and pardon
for those who follow my Way and keep my Word.

But whoever believes in me yet does not keep my Word   15.48
receives no benefit from it, even though he believes in me.
He has run his course in vain.
His end is determined for ruin and punishment of great pain,
for he has failed to follow the Way of God.

16. False Prophets

Beware of false prophets, who come to you in sheep's clothing,   16.1
but inwardly are ravenous wolves.
By their fruits you will know them.

Every good tree brings forth good fruit,   16.2
but a corrupt tree brings forth evil fruit.
A good tree cannot bear bad fruit, nor can a bad tree
bear good fruit. Are not the fingers of the hand alike,
and the ears of corn in a field?

Do not all fruit-bearing trees bear the same fruit?   16.3
Do they all not bring forth fruit according to their nature?
Do men gather grapes from thorn bushes or figs from thistles?
Every tree is known by its fruit.
And every tree that does not bear good fruit
is cut down and thrown into the fire.

A good man out of the good storehouse of his heart   16.4
brings forth good. An evil man
out of the evil storehouse of his heart brings forth evil.
For out of the abundance of the heart the mouth speaks.

Therefore take heed. For many false prophets will appear   16.5
and deceive many. Do not be led astray.
Do not become doubters who serve other gods.

Many will come in my name saying, "I am he,"   16.6
and, "The time has drawn nigh." Do not follow them.
Many will come in my name, saying, "I am Christ."
Believe them not and draw not near.

If they say, "Behold, he is in the desert," do not go forth.   16.7
If they say, "He is in the secret chambers," believe it not.
The Son of God does not come in manifest form.

Lightning that flashes in one part of the sky lights all the rest.   16.8
So will it be with the coming of the Son of Man.
With a host of angels you will see me in the clouds of Heaven

in my glory. With my cross before me I will come
in my glory. Shining seven times as bright as the sun
I will come in my glory.

With all the saints and angels as witnesses, the Father will   16.9
crown my head that I may judge the dead and the living,
and reward or punish every man according to his works.

But first I must suffer many things and be rejected   16.10
by this generation. For wherever the carcass appears,
there the eagles will gather.

So when you hear of wars and great disorder,   16.11
do not be terrified or surprised. These things must come
to pass, and the end will not come soon. Remember the parable
of the fig tree. When its shoots have gone forth and its boughs
have sprouted, the end of the world will come.

Understand that the fig tree is the house of Israel.   16.12
When its boughs have sprouted, the false Christs
will come and awaken false hope, saying, "I am the Christ,
who has now come into the world."

But when men see the wickedness of the false Christs   16.13
they will turn away from them, and deny even him
to whom our Father gave praise, the first Christ,
whom they crucified and sinned against exceedingly.

But the deceiver is not the Christ.   16.14
And when the deceiver is rejected, he will kill with the sword
and there will be many martyrs by his hand.
Then will the boughs of the house of Israel sprout,
and they will be killed and become martyrs.

Enoch and Elias will be sent to tell the house of Israel   16.15
that this is the deceiver who must come into the world
and do signs and wonders in order to deceive.
And that they who are slain by his hand shall be martyrs,
and shall be counted among the good and righteous martyrs
who have pleased God in their life.

So take heed. I have warned you of all things beforehand.   16.16
If anyone says to you, "Look, here is Christ!" do not believe it.
False Christs and false prophets will appear showing signs
and wonders to lead the ignorant astray.
So many signs and wonders that, were it possible,
they might deceive the very elect.

Ignore them. Every plant the Father has not planted   16.17
will be uprooted. They are blind leaders of the blind.
And if a blind man leads a blind man, both fall into a ditch.

A disciple is not greater than his teacher, but everyone   16.18
who is perfectly trained will be as great as his teacher.

There will come other teachings in conflict with my Way,   16.19
and because these teachers seek their own glory
and produce worthless teachings, death will result.
They will turn away from my Word even those
who would follow me, and steal from them eternal Life.

Come, let us fulfill the will of the perfect Father.   16.20
For truly, they are coming who will mete out judgment
to such as these, and they will be put to shame.

But me they cannot touch. Nor you, though you stand   16.21
in their midst. Do not be afraid. Their minds shall be stopped,
for the invisible One opposes them.

Many who oppose Truth and are messengers of error   16.22
will make institutions of their error,
and create false dogma from the purity of my teachings.
They will call themselves bishops and deacons,
as if they have received their authority from God.

Ruling from a narrow perspective,   16.23
thinking Truth and error are the same,
they make a business of my words and create for themselves
a harsh fate. They bend themselves under the judgment
of their own rules. Those people are dry canals.

This nation of immortal souls will continue in vain until 16.24
I come again, and messengers of error will be among them.
For it is my forgiveness of their transgressions—
which befell them through their adversary, Hermas,
first-born of unrighteousness—that liberates them
from slavery and gives them freedom to create an imitation
fragment of me in the name of a dead man, in order that
the Light of All not be known by the mass of men.

But such as these will be cast into outer darkness, 16.25
away from the sons of Light. They shall not enter the Light,
nor shall those who follow such as these.

For those who sin against my commandment— 16.26
who teach something else, who subtract from and add to,
who work for their own glory, alienating those
who rightly believe in me—I will deliver them to ruin.

Many will accept my teachings at first then turn from them. 16.27
It is by the will of the Father that this happens.
Their error is what he commands, so that by his judgment
upon them he may reveal the true servants of the Word.

Those who associate with false prophets have no discernment, 16.28
and will soon become their prisoners.
They will praise these men who propagate falsehood.
They will cleave to the name of a dead man,
thinking it will purify their sin.

But they will be greatly denied. They will fall into great error, 16.29
and into the hands of evil, cunning men.
They will be mired in dogma and ruled by heretics.

Some will blaspheme Truth, proclaim false teachings, 16.30
and say all manner of evil things against each other.
They will proclaim the power of the fallen angels,
and of a naked man and woman who became manifold
and subject to much suffering.

Those who say these things will talk about visions.   16.31
And if they say the visions come from a demon worthy
of such error, they shall receive perdition, not perfection.

It is to the good, guileless, sincere ones   16.32
that the mystery of death is revealed.
They shall know the kingdom of those reborn in Christ.

17. Miscellany

The man old in days will not hesitate to ask a small child   17.1
seven days old about the place of life, and he will live.
For many who are first will become last,
and they will become one and the same.

Have you never read, "Out of the mouths of babes   17.2
and sucklings you have perfected praise"?

Let the children first be filled. It is not good to take   17.3
the children's bread and throw it to dogs.

Bring out from every other house and bring into the house   17.4
of the Father. But do not take anything
from the house of the Father, nor carry it off.

When you were young, you girded yourself   17.5
and walked where you would. But when you are old,
you will stretch out your hands, and another will gird you
and carry you where you do not wish to go.

No one puts a piece of unshrunk cloth on an old garment.   17.6
For the patch pulls away from the garment,
and the tear is made worse.

Nor is new wine put into old wineskins, lest the wineskins spoil   17.7
and burst, and the wine be spilled. Rather, new wine must be
put into new wineskins so both are preserved.

And no one, having drunk old wine, immediately desires   17.8
to drink new wine. He says, "The old wine is better."

Every kingdom divided against itself is brought to   17.9
desolation. A house divided against itself will not stand.

If Satan casts out Satan, he is divided against himself.   17.10
How then will his kingdom stand? If I cast out demons
by Beelzebub, by whom do your sons cast them out?

They shall be your judges. But if I cast out demons by the
Spirit of God, surely the kingdom of God is upon you.

If they call the master of the house Beelzebub,   17.11
how much more will they call those of his household.
Therefore do not fear them. There is nothing covered that will
not be revealed, nothing hidden that will not be known.

Blessed are you, my beloved, because you see these mysteries.   17.12
The Father sent an avenging angel to me, one who had stood
before the Father's throne. And this angel would not go up
because he wished to destroy the power of the world.

When I commanded him to go up, a flame issued   17.13
from his hand, and after he had rent the veil of the temple
he divided it into two parts as a testimony to the children
of Israel for my passion, because they crucified me.

He who believes and is baptized will be saved.   17.14
He who does not believe is condemned.

These signs will accompany those who believe.   17.15
In my name they will cast out demons. They will speak
in new tongues. They will pick up serpents,
and if they drink any deadly thing it will not hurt them.
They will lay their hands on the sick and the sick will recover.

My disciples are like children who have settled   17.16
in a field that is not theirs. When the owners of the field
come and say, "Let us have back our field,"
they will undress in their presence to give it back to them.

When will I become revealed to you?   17.17
When you disrobe without being ashamed,
and place your garments under your feet like little children,
and tread on them. Then will you see the son of the living One,
and you will not be afraid.

If it is my will that a man remain until I come,   17.18
what is that to you? Follow me.

Blessed is the lion that is consumed by man   17.19
and becomes man. Cursed is the man who is consumed
by the lion, and the lion becomes man.

The world does not hate you. It hates me because   17.20
I testify that its works are evil. Go to the feast yourselves.
I am not going to the feast, for my time has not yet fully come.

He who hates me hates my Father also.   17.21
He who is not with me is against me.
He who does not gather with me, scatters abroad.

All cannot accept this saying, but only those who are meant 17.22
to receive it. He who is able to accept it, let him receive it.
There are eunuchs who were born eunuchs
from their mother's womb. There are eunuchs
who were made eunuchs by men. And there are men
who live as eunuchs for the sake of the kingdom of Heaven.
He who is able to accept this, let him accept it.

Attaining to the kingdom of the Father is liken to a woman 17.23
carrying a jar full of meal as she walked the long road
to her home. Along the way, the vessel cracked
and meal began spilling out on the road behind her.

Since the leakage was slight she did not notice,   17.24
and so did nothing to stop it. When she arrived home
and put the vessel down, she saw it was empty.

You who have joined the Perfect, the Light, with the Holy Spirit, 17.25
unite the angels with us also, the images.

What can a man give in return for Life?   17.26

You have answered rightly. Do this and you will live.   17.27

Where there are three gods, they are gods.   17.28
Where there are two or one, I am with him.

You ask who will be your leader when I depart from you.   17.2·
I say to you, wherever you are, go to James the righteous,
for whose sake heaven and earth came into being.

Ask me what you wish, so that I can teach you and show you.   17.3·
For there are still seven days, then I ascend to my Father
and shall no more appear to you in this form.

"Lord, show us the abyss, as you promised us."   17.31
You are not ready to see the abyss, but if you wish it,
I will keep my promise.

[He guided them to a state of Truth and beckoned to the angels.   17.32
The earth rolled up like a papyrus roll and the abyss appeared
to their eyes. When the apostles saw it, they fell on their faces.]
Did I not say it was not good for you?
You must be prepared to behold the abyss.

Compare me to someone and tell me whom I am like.   17.33
"You are like a righteous angel."
"You are like a wise philosopher."
"Master, my mouth is wholly incapable of saying who you are like."

I am not your master. Because you have drunk   17.34
from the bubbling spring that I have measured out,
you have become intoxicated.

Who do you say that I, the Son of Man, am?   17.35
"Some say John the Baptist, some say Elijah,
others say Jeremiah or one of the prophets."

But who do you say that I am?   17.36
"You are the Christ, son of the living God."

Blessed are you, Simon, for flesh and blood has not revealed   17.37
this to you, but our Father in Heaven. I say to you
that you shall be called Peter, and that upon this rock
I will build my church, and Hades shall not prevail against it.

And I will give you the keys to the kingdom of Heaven,   17.38
and whatever you bind on earth will be bound in Heaven,
and whatever you loose on earth will be loosed in Heaven.

A man will set out from Cilicia and journey to Damascus   17.39
in Syria to tear asunder the church you must create.
I will speak to him through you, and he will come quickly.

He will be strong in his faith so that this prophecy may   17.40
be fulfilled: "Behold, out of the land of Syria I will call a new
Jerusalem, and I will subdue Zion and it will be captured.
And the barren one who has no children will be fruitful.
She is called the daughter of my father, but to me
she is my bride. Such is the will of he who sends me."

But I will turn that man aside, that he may not   17.41
go to Damascus and complete his evil plan. And the glory
of the Father will come through him. For after I have gone
to remain with the Father, I will speak to him from Heaven.
All will happen as I have predicted concerning this man.

Tell the vision to no one until the Son of Man is risen   17.42
from the dead. Indeed, "Elijah shall come first
and restore all things." But Elijah has come already.
Yet they did not know him, and did to him as they wished.
Likewise, the Son of Man is about to suffer at their hands.

I have told you many times that they are the blind ones   17.43
who have no guide. If you want to know their blindness,
put your hands upon your eyes and say what you see.

Now lift up your hands and listen to what the priests   17.44
and the people are saying. Prick up your ears and listen
to the things they are saying.

See how they do not know what they are saying.   17.45
They are the sons of their own glory, not my servants,
and they have been put to shame.
I have told you, "Leave the blind alone!"

When the hundred and fiftieth year is complete,   17.46
between Pentecost and Passover,
the coming of the Father will take place.

Do not fear what will not happen to many, but only to a few.   17.47

Every scribe instructed concerning Heaven is like a householder   17.48
who brings out of his treasure things new and old.

Were not all things made by my Word and according to   17.49
the plan of my Father? The spirits were made subject to
Solomon himself. Go therefore, since you have been
commanded to do so in my name, and ask him what you wish.

Go into the village over against you, and you shall find   17.50
an ass tied, and a colt with her. Loose them
and bring them to me. And if anyone says something to you,
tell him, "The Lord has need of them,"
and straightaway he will give them to you.

Already the time has come, brothers, that we should   17.51
leave behind our labor and abide in Repose.
For he who abides in Repose will rest forever.

Why does a man carry a lamb on his shoulders?   17.52
So that he may kill it and eat it.
Look for a place for yourselves within Repose,
lest you become a corpse and be eaten.

Have you seen the company of the fathers?   17.53
As is their rest, so also is the honor and glory of those
who will be persecuted for the sake of righteousness.
I will confess them before my Father in Heaven.

Some have entered the kingdom of Heaven laughing,   17.54
and they have come out.

Love covers a multitude of sins. Love and goodness.   17.55
Love builds up.

As a virgin, as a woman, so is the mystery of resurrection
you have shown to me, you who in the beginning of the world
did institute vain feasts for yourselves, and delighted
in the wantonness of the Gentiles, and behaved
in the same way as those who take pleasure in all this.

17.56

Do you suppose that these Galileans were worse sinners
than all other Galileans because they suffered such things?
I tell you, no. Unless you repent, you will all likewise perish.

17.57

Do not judge by appearances. Judge with right judgment.
Be sober! Do not be deceived!

17.58

O Lord, there are many around the drinking trough,
but there is nothing in the cistern.

17.59

He who has bathed does not need to wash except for his feet
and he is clean all over. You are clean, but not all of you.

17.60

Every plant that the Father in Heaven has not planted
will be plucked out.

17.61

Eat every plant, but that which has bitterness eat not.

17.62

Man, who made me a judge or an arbitrator over you?
You ask me to tell your brothers to divide your father's
possessions with you? Who has made me a divider?
I am not a divider, am I?

17.63

Who touched me? Someone has touched me,
for I perceive that virtue is gone out of me.
I have, Lord, and I have been healed. Forgive me.

17.64

Daughter, be of good comfort. Where are they
who condemn you? Has anyone condemned you?
Likewise, neither do I condemn you.
Your faith has made you whole. Go in peace.

17.65

He who believes in the father and the mother
shall be called the son of a harlot.

17.66

The Son of Man comes as a dyer who throws a multitude   17.67
of different colors into the vat and takes them out all white.

I am able to destroy the temple of God,   17.68
and to build it in again three days.
If I destroy the temple, no other will be able to rebuild it.
If you destroy the temple, in three days I will raise it up.

If you follow my Way and keep my Word,   17.69
these stones will minister to you.
For there are five trees in Paradise that remain undisturbed
summer and winter, and whose leaves do not fall.
Whoever becomes acquainted with them
will not experience death.

Thus we shall fulfill all righteousness.   17.70
Peace to you.

Chapter IV
Parables and Metaphors

The Pearl of Great Price
The Invitation
The True Vine
The Sower
The Good Shepherd
The Bridegroom
The Eye of a Needle
Servants and Masters
Lost and Found

Jesus sometimes spoke in parables to illustrate abstract spiritual ideas, using references and examples that could be understood by the masses of his day—family, farming, fishing, livelihood, marriage. It was, and is, an effective teaching device. To this day the parables and metaphors of Jesus are perhaps the most quoted and remembered passages in his teachings. But the true power of these parables is not just that they can be understood by the common man, but that they contain multiple layers of meaning that continue to resonate with even the most dedicated and experienced spiritual practitioners.

In Zen the student is advised to always keep "beginner's mind." That is, never think that you have made "progress" on the spiritual path, but to approach every new day, every new experience, every new moment, as if you know nothing.

Yes, the parables of Jesus have been the source of numerous retellings and may seem old hat to some, but when approached with beginner's mind, all things become new.

18. The Pearl of Great Price

I speak to you in parables because looking, you do not see,   18.1
listening, you do not hear. Nor do you understand.

With what can we compare the kingdom of God?   18.2
What parable shall we use for it?

The kingdom of God is like a mustard seed,   18.3
which is the smallest of all the seeds on earth.
Yet when it falls onto prepared soil it becomes greater
than all the herbs, and produces a great tree,
and the birds of the air flock to nest in its braches.

The kingdom of God is like leaven hidden in dough,   18.4
so that it might rise and be made into many loaves.

The kingdom of God is like treasure hidden   18.5
in a man's land but he does not know about it.
And when he dies, his son inherits the land, but likewise
the son does not know about the treasure, so he sells the land.
But the man who buys the land works it and finds the treasure,
and has money to lend to whomever he will.

Attaining the kingdom of God is like the way of the merchant   18.6
seeking beautiful pearls, who, when he finds
the one pearl of great price, sells all that he has and buys it.

Or like the way of the fisherman who cast his net into the sea   18.7
and drew it up full of small fish. But among them he found
a fine large fish, which the wise fisherman chose
without difficulty, and threw all the small fish back into the sea.

Or like the way of a man who finds treasure hidden in a field,   18.8
and for his joy over it sells all that he has and buys that field.
You, too, seek God's unfailing and enduring treasure,
which no moth comes near to devour and no worm can destroy.

For whoever does not forsake all that he has,   18.9
is not a disciple of my Way.

Attaining the kingdom of God is like the way   18.10
of a certain man who wanted to kill a powerful foe.
First he drew his sword in his own house and stuck it into
the wall, that he might know whether or not his hand
could carry through. Then he slew the powerful foe.

What king, going to war against another king, does not first   18.11
consider whether he is able with ten thousand men
to meet a king who comes against him with twenty thousand?
Else, while the army is still a great way off,
he might send a delegation and ask conditions of peace.

And which of you, intending to build a tower,   18.12
does not first count the cost, whether he has enough to finish?
Lest, after he has laid the foundation, he is not able
to complete the task, and all who see it mock him, saying,
"This man began to build but was not able to finish."

19. The Invitation

The way of God is like the parable of a certain king   19.1
who arranged a feast for the wedding of his son
and sent out a servant to call those who were invited.
"Tell those who are invited I have prepared a feast for them.
My oxen and fatted cattle are killed, and all things are ready.
Come to the wedding."

So the servant went to the first man and said,   19.2
"My lord invites you." But the one invited said,
"I cannot come. I have business with some merchants
and must give them my claims and orders."

He went to another and said, "My lord invites you."   19.3
But the one invited said, "I have just bought a house
and am required there. I do not have any spare time."

He went to another and said, "My lord invites you."   19.4
But the one invited said, "My friend is going to get married,
and I am to prepare the dinner. I shall not be able to come."

He went to another and said, "My lord invites you."   19.5
But the one invited said, "I have inherited a farm
and am on my way to collect rent. I must ask to be excused."

He went to another and said, "My lord invites you."   19.6
But the one invited said, "I have bought five yoke of oxen,
and I must go test them. I cannot accept the invitation."
So it was that one by one all those invited made their excuses.

When the servant returned and reported these things,   19.7
the king became angry and said, "The wedding feast is ready
but those invited are not worthy. Go therefore
into the streets and alleys of the city. Bring in the poor,
the maimed, the lame and the blind."

And when the servant returned, saying, "Lord, it is done   19.8
as you commanded, and still there is room," the king said,
"Then go out into the countryside and fields. Bid everyone
you see to come, that my house may be filled. I tell you,
none of those first invited shall taste my supper."

But when the king came in to see the guests,   19.9
he saw a man there who did not have on a wedding garment.
The king said to him, "Friend, why did you come in here
without a wedding garment?" And the man was speechless.

So the king said to the servants, "Bind him hand and foot.   19.10
Take him away and cast him into outer darkness.
There will be weeping and gnashing of teeth."

For many are called, but few are chosen.   19.11

20. The True Vine

No one gathers figs from thorns nor grapes from thistles.　　20.1
That which is always becoming, is in that from which it is.

If it is from that which is false and evil,　　20.2
it becomes the destruction of the soul, and death.
But the soul that comes to be in the eternal One,
becomes the One, and attains the immortality of Life.

I am the true vine and the Father is the vinedresser.　　20.3
Every branch of mine that does not bear fruit he takes away,
and every branch that does bear fruit he tends,
that it may bear even more fruit.

You are already made clean by the Word I have given you.　　20.4
Abide in me, and I will abide in you.
As a branch cannot bear fruit unless it abides in the vine,
neither can you bear fruit unless you abide in me.

I am the vine and you are the branches.　　20.5
He who abides in me, and I in him, shall bear much fruit,
but apart from me you can do nothing.

For if a man does not abide in me,　　20.6
his branch is cast off and let wither.
And the cast-off branches are thrown into the fire.

The sun and the moon give a fragrance to you,　　20.7
along with the air and spirit, earth and water.
For if the sun does not shine upon these bodies,
they will wither and perish just like weeds or grass.

If the sun shines on the weeds, they prevail　　20.8
and choke the grapevine. But if the grapevine prevails
and shades those weeds and the other brush alongside,
it spreads and flourishes, and it alone inherits the land.

And when it grows up, it dominates all the land it shades   20.9
and is bountiful for its master, and it pleases him even more,
for he would have suffered on account of the weeds and brush
until he uprooted them. But the grapevine alone
shaded and choked them, and they died and became soil.

21. The Sower

Listen: A sower went out to sow. And as he sowed, 21.1
some seed fell by the wayside and the birds came
and devoured it. Other seed fell on rocky ground
where it had not much soil. It immediately sprang up
because it had no depth of earth. But when the sun rose
it was scorched, and it withered because it had no roots.

Other seed fell among thorns, and the thorns grew up and 21.2
choked it, and it yielded no grain. But other seeds fell into good
soil and brought forth grain, growing and increasing and
yielding, thirtyfold and sixtyfold and a hundredfold.

When someone hears the Word of the Kingdom 21.3
and does not understand it, Satan comes quickly
and snatches away what was sown in his heart.
This is he who received seed by the wayside.

He who received the seed on rocky ground is one who 21.4
hears the Word and immediately receives it with joy,
yet has no root in himself, so it does not endure.
For when tribulation or persecution arises because of the Word,
immediately he stumbles.

He who received seed among the thorns is he who 21.5
hears the Word, but the cares of this world
and the deceitfulness of riches choke out the Word,
and he becomes unfruitful.

But he who received seed on the good soil is he who 21.6
hears the Word and understands it and keeps it.
These are the ones who bear fruit and produce,
some thirtyfold, some sixtyfold, some a hundredfold.

Become earnest about the Word! 21.7
For as to the Word, the first part is faith,
the second is love, the third is works.
From these come Life.

For the Word is like a grain of wheat. When someone
sows it he has faith in it. And when it sprouts, he loves it
because he sees many grains in place of one. And when he
works he is saved because he prepares the grain for food,
and also leaves some to sow as seed.

21.8

It is in this way that you enter the kingdom of Heaven.
But unless you receive it yourself, through direct knowing,
you will not be able to find it.

21.9

I tell you this, that you may know yourself.
The kingdom of Heaven is like an ear of grain
after it has sprouted in a field. When it has ripened,
it scatters its fruit and again fills the field with grain.
Even so, hasten to reap the grain of Life for yourself,
that you may be filled with the Kingdom!

21.10

For the kingdom of God is as if a man should scatter seed
upon the ground, and should sleep and rise night and day,
and the seed should sprout and grow, he knows not how.
The earth produces of itself, first the blade, then the ear,
then the full grain in the ear. But when the grain is ripe
he at once takes up his sickle because the harvest has come.

21.11

Do not think there are yet four months until the harvest.
I tell you, lift up your eyes and see.
The fields are already white for harvest.

21.12

He who reaps receives bounty and gathers fruit for eternal Life,
so that sower and reaper may rejoice together.
Here the saying holds true, "One sows and another reaps."
I send you to reap that for which you did not labor.
Others have labored, and you have entered into their labor.

21.13

The harvest is truly plentiful, but the reapers are few.
Therefore pray to the Lord to send reapers into his harvest.

21.14

Let there be among you a man of understanding,
who, when the grain has ripened, comes quickly
with his sickle in hand and reaps it.

21.15

For the kingdom of Heaven is like the parable of a man   21.16
who sowed good seed into his field, but at night
his enemy came and sowed weeds among the wheat.
And when the grain sprouted, weeds also appeared.

So his servants said to him, "Sir, did you not sow good seed   21.17
in your field? How then does it have weeds?"
He said to them, "An enemy has done this."
The servants said, "Do you want us to gather them up?"

But the owner said, "No, lest while you gather up the weeds   21.18
you also uproot the wheat. Let both grow together
until the harvest. At the harvest I will say to the reapers,
"First gather the weeds and bind them in bundles to burn,
then gather the good wheat into my barn.'"

He who sows the good seed is the Son of Man.   21.19
The field is the world.
The good seeds are the sons of the Kingdom.
The weeds are the sons of the wicked one,
and the enemy who sowed them is Satan.

The harvest is the end of the age, and the reapers are the angels.   21.20
As the weeds are gathered and burned in the fire,
likewise will it be at the end of the age.

The Son of Man will send out his angels, and they will gather   21.21
out of this realm all those who practice lawlessness and all
things that offend. And they will be cast into the furnace of fire.
There will be wailing and gnashing of teeth.

Then righteous will shine forth like the sun   21.22
in the kingdom of the Father.

Do not allow the kingdom of Heaven to wither.   21.23
It is like a palm tree whose fruit has poured down
around it and sent forth shoots, which after they have sprouted
cause the pith to dry up.

So it is also with the fruit grown from this single root.   21.24
When it is picked the fruit is borne home by many.
The root is certainly good, and in order to produce new plants,
you now must find it.

Consider the seeds of wheat. As something dry   21.25
and without a soul does a man sow them in the earth,
to live again and bear fruit.

And the earth gives them back as a pledge entrusted to it.   21.26
For unless a grain of wheat falls into the earth and dies,
it remains alone. But if it dies, it bears much fruit.

This which dies, this which is sown as seed in the earth   21.27
to become alive and be restored to life, is man.
How much more shall God raise up on the day of decision
those who believe in him and are chosen by him
and for whom he made the earth?

All this shall the earth give back on the day of decision.   21.28
For the earth shall also be judged, and heaven with it.

22. The Good Shepherd

I am the door of the sheepfold. All who came before me   22.1
were thieves and robbers, but the sheep did not heed them.
I am the door. Anyone who enters by me will be saved,
and will go in and out and find pasture.

The thief comes only to steal and kill and destroy.   22.2
I come that you may have life, and have it abundantly.
I am the good shepherd.
The good shepherd lays down his life for the sheep.

He who does not enter the sheepfold by the door   22.3
but climbs in by another way is a thief and a robber.
He who enters by the door is the shepherd of the sheep.
To him the gatekeeper opens.

The sheep hear his voice, and he calls his own sheep by name   22.4
and leads them out. And when he has brought out all his own
he goes before them, and the sheep follow him, for they know
his voice. A stranger they will not follow, but will flee
from him, for they do not know the voice of strangers.

They flee because he is a hireling and cares nothing   22.5
for the sheep. I am the good shepherd. I know my own
and my own know me, just as the Father knows me
and I know the Father. I lay down my life for the sheep.

And I have other sheep that are not of this fold.   22.6
I must bring them also, and they will heed my voice.
There shall be one flock, one shepherd.

The Father loves me because I lay down my life,   22.7
that I may take it up again. No one takes it from me.
I lay it down of my own accord. I have the power
to lay it down, and I have the power to take it up again.
This power I receive from the Father.

My sheep hear my voice. I know them and they follow me.   22.8
I give them eternal Life and they shall never perish.
No one shall snatch them out of my hand.
The Father, who has given them to me, is greater than all.
No one is able to snatch them out of the Father's hand.

But whoever is shut out is shut out.   22.9
Insight, Knowledge, Obedience, Endurance, Mercy.
These have slept even in those who believe in me
and acknowledge me.

And because those in whom these slept did not follow   22.10
my Way, they will be outside the Kingdom and the fold
of the shepherd. And whoever remains outside the fold
will the wolf eat.

For although he hears, he will be judged and will die.   22.11
Much suffering and distress will come upon him,
and he will have much to endure.

And although he is greatly pained, and cut into pieces,   22.12
and lacerated with long and painful punishment,
he will not die quickly.

23. The Bridegroom

The way of God is like the parable of the ten virgins   23.1
who took their lamps and went out to meet the bridegroom.
Five of them were wise, and five were foolish.
Those who were foolish took no vessels of oil
for their lamps. The wise took vessels of oil with them.
And so it was that the bridegroom was delayed,
so while they waited they slept.

Then at midnight a cry was heard.   23.2
"Behold, the bridegroom is coming. Go out to meet him!"
And the ten virgins arose and trimmed their lamps.
And the foolish said to the wise, "Give us some of your oil
for our lamps are going out." But the wise answered,
"No, lest there should not be enough for us.
Go to those who sell, and buy oil for yourselves."

While they were gone to buy oil the bridegroom came,   23.3
and those who were ready went in with him to the wedding,
and the door was shut. Later the foolish virgins
came and knocked, saying, "Lord, Lord, open to us!"
But he answered them and said, "Truly, I do not know you."

Watch therefore, and be ready. You know neither the day   23.4
nor the hour the Son of Man will come.

"Lord, let us fast and pray today."   23.5
What sin have I have committed?
Where have I been defeated? When the bridegroom
leaves the bridal chamber, then you can fast and pray.

Shall the friends of the bridegroom lament while   23.6
the bridegroom is yet with them? The day will come when
the bridegroom will be taken from them. Then let them fast.

Many are standing at the door, but it is the solitary   23.7
who will enter the bridal chamber.

I tell you this that you may do as I have done to you.   23.8
Be like the five wise virgins who kindled their light
and did not slumber, who went with their lamps to meet
the lord, the bridegroom, and went with him into the
bridegroom's house. Be not like the five foolish ones
who were not able to keep watch, but fell asleep.

The five wise are called by the prophet, daughters of God,   23.9
whose names let men hear: Faith, Love, Joy, Peace, Hope.
As soon as they who believe in me have these, they will
be leaders to those who believe in me, and in him who sent me.

I am the Lord and I am the bridegroom.   23.10
The wise have received me and have gone with me
into the house of the bridegroom, and sat down at the table
of the bridegroom, and rejoiced.

But the foolish slept. And when they awoke they went   23.11
to the house of the bridegroom and knocked at the doors,
for they were shut. And they wept because they were shut out.

24. The Eye of a Needle

There was a certain rich man clothed in purple and fine linen   24.1
who fared sumptuously every day. And there was a certain
beggar named Lazarus, full of sores, who lay at the rich man's
gate desiring to be fed with the crumbs that fell from his table.
And as he lay there, dogs came and licked at his sores.

Soon, the beggar died and was carried by angels   24.2
to Abraham's bosom. Soon after, the rich man also died
and was buried, and fell into torment in Hades,
where he lifted up his eyes and saw Abraham afar off,
and he saw Lazarus in Abraham's bosom.

And he cried out and said, "Father, have mercy on me.   24.3
Send Lazarus that he may dip the tip of his finger in water
and cool my tongue, for I am tormented in this flame."

But Abraham said, "Son, remember that in your lifetime   24.4
you received good things, and likewise Lazarus evil things.
But now he is comforted and you are tormented.

And besides, between us and you there is a great gulf,   24.5
so that those who want to pass from here to you cannot,
nor can those from there pass to us."

So the rich man said, "I beg you therefore, Father Abraham,   24.6
that you send him to my father's house, for I have five brothers,
that he may testify to them, lest they also come to
this place of torment." Abraham said, "They have Moses
and the prophets. Let your brothers hear them."

The rich man said, "No Father, they cannot hear them,   24.7
but if one comes to them from the dead, they will repent."
But Abraham said, "If they cannot hear Moses
and the prophets, neither will they be persuaded
though one rises from the dead."

There was another rich man whose land yielded plentifully   24.8
and he had many goods. He thought, "Since I no longer have
room to store all my crops, I will tear down my barns
and build greater barns, and there I will store
all my crops and my goods.

And I will say to my soul, 'Soul, you have goods   24.9
and money laid up for many years. Take your ease.
Eat, drink, and be merry.'"

Such were his intentions. But God said to him,   24.10
"Fool! This night your soul may be required of you.
Then who will enjoy all those things you have stored?"
And that same night he died.

So it is with anyone who lays up earthly treasure for himself   24.11
and is not rich with God.

Whoever finds the world and becomes rich,   24.12
let him renounce the world.

For if you do not fast as regards the world,   24.13
you will not find the Kingdom.
If you do not observe the Sabbath as the Sabbath,
you will not see the Father.

How hard it is for a rich man to enter the Kingdom!   24.14
It is easier for a camel to pass through the eye of a needle
than for a rich man to enter the kingdom of God.

25. Servants and Masters

A man cannot mount two horses or stretch two bows,   25.1
nor can a servant serve two masters.
For he will either love one and hate the other,
or honor the one and treat the other with contempt.
You cannot serve both God and mammon.

When a man leaves home for a journey   25.2
he puts his servants in charge, each with his work,
and commands the doorkeeper to be on the watch.

Who then is like the wise and faithful servant   25.3
whom his master makes steward of his household
when he journeys, to give them sustenance in due season?
Blessed is that servant whom his master finds so doing
when he returns. Truly, he will make him ruler
over all his domain.

But if that servant is evil and thinks, "My master   25.4
will not soon return," and beats the other servants,
and eats and drinks with the drunken,
the master of that servant will come on a day
he does not expect him, and at an hour
for which he is unprepared.

And he will cut that servant in two and appoint him   25.5
his portion with the hypocrites.
There will be weeping and gnashing of teeth.

The servant who knows his master's will   25.6
yet does not prepare himself, or do according to his will,
shall be beaten with many stripes.

But the servant who does not know his master's will yet   25.7
commits acts deserving of stripes, shall be beaten with few.

For everyone to whom much is given, from him,   25.8
much is required. And to him to whom much is committed,
of him, more will be asked.

For the way of God can be seen in the parable of a nobleman   25.9
who called his servants to him and gave them money
to do business for him. To one he gave five talents,
to another two and to another one —
to each according to his own ability.
Then he immediately went on a journey to a far country.

But so it was also that his citizens hated him,   25.10
and when he had gone they sent a delegation to his house,
saying, "We will not have this man reign over us."

Now he who received the five talents traded with them,   25.11
and made another five talents for his master.
And he who received two talents used them
to gain two more. But he who received one talent
dug a hole in the ground and hid his lord's money.

After a long time the lord of those servants returned   25.12
and settled accounts with them. He who had received
five talents brought five more talents, saying,
"Lord, you delivered to me five talents, and look,
I have gained five more talents besides."

And his lord said, "Well done, good and faithful servant.   25.13
You were faithful over a few things so I will make you
ruler over many things. Enter into the joy of your lord."

He who had received two talents came and said,   25.14
"Lord, you delivered to me two talents, and look,
I have gained two more talents besides."

And his lord said, "Well done, good and faithful servant.   25.15
You were faithful over a few things so I will make you
ruler over many things. Enter into the joy of your lord."

Then he who had received one talent came and said,   25.16
"Lord, I knew you to be a hard businessman,
collecting where you have not deposited,
reaping where you have not sown. And I was afraid
of losing what you gave me so I hid your talent in the ground.
Look, there you have back what is yours."

And his lord said, "You are an ignorant and lazy servant.   25.17
Out of your own mouth I judge you.
You knew that I collect where I have not deposited,
that I reap where I have not scattered seed.
Why did you not deposit my money with bankers
so that upon my return I would receive it back with interest?

"Take the talent from him. Give it to him who has five talents.   25.18
Cast this unprofitable servant into outer darkness,
where there will be weeping and gnashing of teeth.
Then bring here the citizens who did not want me to
reign over them, and slay these enemies before me."

And so it is that to everyone who has,   25.19
more will be given and he will have abundance.
But from him who does not have,
even what little is his will be taken away.

For if you cannot keep to what is little,   25.20
who will give you what is great?
He who is faithful in what is least, is faithful also in much.

Truly, to everyone who has it will be given to him   25.21
and he will have plenty. But he who does not have—
that is, the man of this earthly place, who is completely dead,
who is alienated from the ground of Creation, who,
if the One of immortal essence appears, thinks that he stands
apart and apprehends Him—it will be taken from
this man of poverty and be added unto the one who has.

The way of God can be heard in another parable.   25.22
There was a certain landowner who planted a vineyard.
He set a hedge around it, dug a winepress, and built a tower.
Then he leased it to vinedressers and went into a far country.

When vintage-time drew near he sent his servants to the   25.23
vineyard, that they might receive its fruit. The vinedressers
beat one of the servants, stoned another and killed a third.
So the landowner sent other servants, more than the first time,
but the vinedressers did likewise to them. Then finally
he sent his son to them, saying, "They will respect my son."

But when the vinedressers saw the son   25.24
they said among themselves, "This is the heir.
Let us kill him and seize his inheritance."
So they took him out of the vineyard and killed him.

Now, when the owner of the vineyard comes with power,   25.25
what do you think he will he do to those vinedressers?
If you say he will destroy those wicked men
and lease his vineyard to men who will render unto him
the fruits in their seasons, you have answered rightly.

What man, having a servant out plowing or tending sheep,   25.26
says to him when he returns from the field,
"Come at once and sit down to eat"? Rather he will say,
"Prepare something for my supper, and gird yourself
and serve me until I have eaten and drunk.
Afterward you will eat and drink."

And does the master thank the servant because he does that   25.27
which is commanded of him? I think not. Therefore you,
when you do those things that are commanded of you, say only,
"I am but an unprofitable servant. I do what is my duty to do."

Let your waist be girded and your lamps burning.   25.28
Be like men who wait for their master to return
from the wedding, that when he comes and knocks
you may open to him immediately.

Blessed are those servants whom the master, when he comes,   25.29
finds faithfully watching. I tell you he will gird himself
and have them sit down to eat, and will himself serve them.
And if he should come in the second watch or in the third
and find them so, blessed indeed are those servants.

For the way of Heaven is like the parable of the landowner   25.30
who went out early in the morning to hire laborers
for his vineyard. He agreed with the laborers to pay them
a denarius a day and sent them to work in his vineyard.

Then he went out about the third hour and saw others 25.31
standing idle in the marketplace, and said to them,
"You also go work in my vineyard, and whatever is right
I will pay you." So they went.

Again he went out about the sixth hour and the ninth hour, 25.32
and did likewise. And about the eleventh hour he went out
and found others standing idle. And he said to them,
"Why have you been standing here idle all day?"
They said, "Because no one hired us."
So he said to them, "You also go work in the vineyard,
and whatever is right you will receive."

Now when evening came, the owner of the vineyard 25.33
said to his steward, "Call the laborers and give them their
wages, beginning with the last to the first."

When those who were hired about the eleventh hour came, 25.34
each received a denarius. So when the first to be hired came,
they supposed that they would receive more.
But they likewise each received a denarius.

And they complained to the landowner, saying, "These last 25.35
men have worked only one hour, yet you made them equal
to us who have borne the burden and the heat of the day."

The landowner answered one of them, saying, 25.36
"Friend, I am doing you no wrong. Did you not agree
with me for a denarius? Take what is yours and go your way.
I wish to give to this last man the same as to you.
Is it not lawful for me to do what I wish with my own things?
Or is your eye evil because I am good?"

So it is that the last will be first, and the first will be last. 25.37
For many are called, but few are chosen.

Listen to the parable of a rich man who had a steward, 25.38
and an accusation was brought to him that the steward
was wasting his goods. So he called the steward and said
to him, "What is this I hear about you? You can no longer
be steward. Bring me an accounting of your stewardship."

The steward thought, "What shall I do? My master is taking   25.39
the stewardship from me. I cannot dig dirt for a living,
and I am ashamed to beg." So he resolved a plan
for what to do so that others would receive him into
their houses after he was put out of the stewardship.

He called every one of his master's debtors to him,   25.40
and said to the first, "How much do you owe my master?"
And he was told, "A hundred measures of oil."
So the steward said to him, "Take your bill, and write fifty."
Then he said to another, "How much do you owe?"
And he was told, "A hundred measures of wheat." So the
steward said to him, "Take your bill, and write eighty."

Yet when the master heard of this he commended   25.41
the dishonest steward because he had dealt shrewdly.
For the sons of this world are more shrewd
in their generation than are the sons of Light.

26. Lost and Found

The Way of God is like the parable of a certain man 26.1
who had two sons. The younger of them said to his father,
"Father, give me the portion of your goods that falls to me."
So the man divided his goods between his two sons.

Not many days after, the younger son gathered 26.2
all that he had and journeyed to a far country,
and there wasted his goods with prodigal living.

But after he had spent all, there arose a famine in that land, 26.3
and he began to be in want. So he joined himself to a citizen
of that country, who sent him into his fields to feed swine.
And the son would gladly have filled his stomach with
the pods the swine ate, but no one gave him anything.

And when he came to himself, he thought, 26.4
"My father's hired servants have bread enough to spare,
yet I perish with hunger! I will go to my father
and say to him, 'Father, I have sinned against Heaven
and in your sight, and am no longer worthy to be called
your son. Make me like one of your hired servants.'"

So he arose and went to his father. And when he was still 26.5
a great way off his father saw him and felt compassion,
and ran to him and fell on his neck and kissed him.
And the son said, "Father, I have sinned against Heaven
and in your sight. I am not worthy to be called your son."

But the father said to his servants, "Bring out the best robe 26.6
and put it on him. Put a ring on his hand,
and sandals on his feet. Bring out the fatted calf and kill it.
Let us eat and be merry. For my son was dead
and now he lives. He was lost and now is found."
And they began to be merry.

Now his older son was in the field. And as he came   26.7
and drew near to the house, he heard music and dancing.
So he called one of the servants and asked
what these things meant. The servant said, "Your brother
has come home, and because your father has received him
safe and sound, he has killed the fatted calf."

The older son became angry at this and would not go in.   26.8
So his father came out and pleaded with him.
And he said to his father, "Lo, these many years I have been
serving you. I never transgressed your commandment
at any time, yet you never gave me even a young goat
that I might make merry with my friends.
But when your other son returns, who has devoured
your livelihood with harlots, you kill the fatted calf for him."

His father said, "Son, you are always with me,   26.9
and all that I have is yours. But it is right
that we make merry and be glad, for your brother was dead
and is alive again. He was lost, yet now is found."

For what man, having a hundred sheep, if he loses one,   26.10
does not leave the ninety-nine and go after the one
that is lost, and when he has found it,
lift it onto his shoulders, rejoicing?

Assuredly, he rejoices more over that sheep   26.11
than over the ninety-nine that did not go astray.
And having gone to such trouble, he says to the sheep,
"I care for you more than the ninety-nine."

Likewise, it is not the will of the Father that even one   26.12
of his little ones should perish. Truly, there will be more joy
in Heaven over one sinner who repents than over ninety-nine
just persons who need no repentance.

Or what woman, having ten silver coins, if she loses one coin   26.13
does not light a lamp, sweep the house, and search carefully
until she finds it? And when she has found it, call her friends
and neighbors together, saying, "Rejoice with me,
for I have found the coin that I lost!" Likewise, there is great joy
among the angels of God over one sinner who repents.

Listen: There was a certain creditor who had two debtors.   26.14
One owed him five hundred denarii and the other fifty.
And when they had nothing with which to repay him,
he freely forgave them both.

So which of them do you think will love him more?   26.15
If you suppose the one whom he forgave more,
then you have rightly judged.

A man had two sons, and he went to the first and said,   26.16
"Son, go work today in my vineyard." The son answered,
"No, I will not," but afterward regretted it and went.
Then he went to the second son and said likewise.
And he answered, "Yes sir, I will go," but he did not go.

So what do you think? Which of the two sons did the will   26.17
of his father? The first, certainly. Even tax collectors and
harlots shall enter the kingdom of God before the second son.

If you knock upon a friend's door at midnight and say,   26.18
"Friend, lend me three loaves, for a guest has arrived
and I have nothing to set before him."
And your friend answers from within, saying,
"Do not trouble me. My door is shut, and my children
are with me in bed. I cannot rise and give to you."

I say to you, that even though he will not rise and give to you   26.19
because he is your friend, if you persist, he will rise and give
you as many loaves as you need because of your persistence.

Likewise, there was a certain judge who did not fear God   26.20
nor regard man. And there was a widow in his city who came
often to him, saying, "Get justice for me from my adversary."

And for awhile he would not. But then he thought,   26.21
"I do not fear God nor regard man,
yet because this widow troubles me I will get justice for her,
lest by her continual coming she weary me."

Hear well what this unjust judge said. Like this,   26.22
will not God grant mercy for his own elect who cry out
day and night to him, though he bears long with them?
I tell you that he will grant them mercy with great speed.

Yet when the Son of Man comes, will he find faith on the earth?   26.23

Chapter V
Destiny

O Jerusalem
Dance of Praise
Last Supper
Crucifixion
Resurrection

The sermons in Part V include sayings relevant to the events surrounding Jesus' death and resurrection. He rails against Jerusalem, the city he knows will kill him. He gathers his disciples for a final meal. He allows himself to be arrested, tried and tortured. He suffers death on the cross, and on the third day he rises up again. And all the while, he teaches.

It would be difficult to imagine a more emotional and dramatic end to a great life. No death in history is more recognizable and remembered, and for much of the world, time itself is marked by a calendar keyed to the crucifixion of Jesus. The passion of Christ has been told hundreds of times in books and movies, yet we still find it moving and compelling.

It's an incredible story that by its power alone has drawn millions to convert to Christianity. The image of Jesus crucified is displayed in countless homes and buildings and vehicles around the world, and the cross on which he died has become a ubiquitous symbol, not just of the Christian church, but of a force that can hold back evil and exorcize devils from the possessed.

Yet perhaps its greatest power is as a metaphor for those who seek to follow the example of Jesus and become like him. Eternal Life, it seems, is not bestowed upon the uncommitted and faint-hearted. It comes to those who are willing to pay the price — which is not less than everything.

Truly, he who loves his life shall lose it.
But he who renounces his life in this world,
shall know eternal Life.

27. O Jerusalem

I was sent to save the lost sheep of the house of Israel,   27.1
and I must preach the kingdom of God to other nations also,
because for this purpose I have come into the world.

And whoever is ashamed of me and my words   27.2
in this adulterous and sinful generation,
of him will the Son of Man also be ashamed
when he comes in the glory of the Father with his holy angels.

To what shall I liken the men of this generation? They are like   27.3
children in the marketplace, calling out to one another.
"We played the flute for you and you did not dance.
We mourned to you and you did not weep."

O Jerusalem, Jerusalem, the one who kills the prophets   27.4
and stones those who are sent to her.
How often I have wanted to gather your children together,
as a hen gathers her brood under her wings.

But you were not willing, and your house   27.5
is now left to you desolate. Truly, you shall not see me
until the time comes when you say,
"Blessed is he who comes in the name of God."

God also said, "I will send them prophets and apostles,   27.6
and some of them they will persecute and kill."
The blood of all the prophets shed from the foundation
of the world until now may be required of this generation—
from the blood of Abel to the blood of Zechariah,
who perished between the altar and the temple.
Yes, I say to you, it shall be required of this generation.

This is an evil generation. It seeks a sign, and no sign   27.7
will be given to it except the sign of Jonah the prophet.
For as Jonah became a sign to the Ninevites,
so also the Son of Man will be to this generation.

When it is evening you say, "It will be fair weather tomorrow,   27.8
for the sky is red," and in the morning, "It will be foul weather
today, for the sky is red and threatening." Hypocrites!
You know how to discern the face of the sky,
but you cannot discern the signs of the times!

Believe me, the hour is coming   27.9
when neither on this mountain nor in Jerusalem
will you worship the Father.

Have you never read in the scriptures: "The stone that   27.10
the builders rejected has become the head cornerstone.
This was the Lord's doing, and it is marvelous in our eyes"?

Therefore I say, the kingdom of God will be taken from you   27.11
and given to a nation bearing the fruits of it.
And whoever falls on this stone will be broken,
and whomever it falls upon, will be ground to powder.

Listen: A certain man had a fig tree in his garden,   27.12
and for years he came seeking fruit on it and found none.
So he said to the keeper of his garden, "For many years
I have come seeking fruit on this tree but find none.
Why does it use up the ground? Cut it down."

But the keeper said, "Sir, let it alone for one more year.   27.13
I will dig the ground around it and fertilize it,
and if it bears fruit, well. If not, I will immediately
cut it down and plant another one in its place."

Understand that the fig tree is the house of Israel,   27.14
and already the ax is laid at the root.

O faithless and perverse generation,   27.15
how long shall I be with you?
How long shall I bear with you?

He who is not with me is against me.   27.16
He who does not gather with me, scatters.

When an unclean spirit goes out of a man
he goes through dry places, seeking rest. Finding none,
he says, "I will return to my house from which I came."

27.17

And when he returns he finds it empty, clean,
and put in order. Yet if he brings with him seven other spirits,
more wicked than the first, and they enter and dwell there,
that man's state is worse than before.
So shall it be with this wicked generation.

27.18

Take heed, and beware of the leaven
of the Pharisees and the Sadducees.

27.19

Beware of the leaven of the Pharisees, which is hypocrisy.
For there is nothing covered that will not be revealed,
nothing hidden that will not be known.

27.20

Whatever you have spoken in the dark
will be heard in the light. What you have whispered in the ear
in inner rooms, will be proclaimed on the housetops.

27.21

Brood of vipers! How can you, being evil, speak good?
For out of the abundance of the heart the mouth speaks.

27.22

A good man out of the good treasure of his heart
brings forth good things. An evil man
out of the evil treasure of his heart brings forth evil things.

27.23

Beware of the scribes, who like to go about in long robes,
and have salutations in the market places, and the best seats
in the synagogues, and the places of honor at feasts.

27.24

Woe to you, scribes and Pharisees. Hypocrites!
For you devour widows' houses,
and for a pretense make long prayers.
Therefore you will receive greater condemnation.

27.25

Woe to you, scribes and Pharisees! Hypocrites!
For you shut up the kingdom of Heaven against men.
You neither go in yourselves, nor do you allow
those who would enter to go in.

27.26

Woe to you, scribes and Pharisees! Hypocrites!   27.27
For you travel land and sea to win one proselyte,
and when he is won, you make him
twice as much a son of Hell as yourselves.

Woe to you, scribes and Pharisees! Hypocrites!   27.28
You pay tithe of mint and anise and cumin, yet neglect
the weightier matters of the law: justice, mercy, and faith.
These you ought to do, without leaving the others undone.
Blind guides, who strain out a gnat and swallow a camel!

Woe to you, scribes and Pharisees! Hypocrites!   27.29
For you cleanse the outside of the cup and dish,
but inside you are full of extortion and self-indulgence.
Blind Pharisee, first cleanse the inside of the cup and dish,
that the outside of them may be clean also.

Why do you wash the outside of the cup?   27.30
Do you not realize that he who made the inside
is the same one who made the outside?

Woe to you, scribes and Pharisees! Hypocrites!   27.31
You are like whitewashed tombs that outwardly
appear beautiful, but inside are full of dead men's bones
and all uncleanness. You outwardly appear righteous to men,
but inside you are full of hypocrisy and lawlessness.

Woe to you, scribes and Pharisees! Hypocrites!   27.32
Because you build the tombs of the prophets
and adorn the monuments of the righteous, and say,
"If we had lived in the days of our fathers, we would not
have been partakers with them in the blood of the prophets."

Therefore you are witnesses against yourselves,   27.33
that you are sons of those who murdered the prophets.
Fill up, then the measure of your fathers' guilt.
Serpents! Brood of vipers!
How can you escape the condemnation of Hell?

Woe to you, blind guides, who say, "Whoever swears
by the altar, it is nothing, but whoever swears by the gift
that is on it, he is obliged to perform it." Blind fools!
Which is greater, the gift or the altar that sanctifies the gift?

27.34

He who swears by the altar, swears by it
and by all things on it. He who swears by the temple,
swears by it and by him who dwells in it.
He who swears by Heaven, swears by the throne of God
and the One who sits on it.

27.35

You have a fine way of rejecting the commandment of God
in order to keep your tradition! Moses said,
"Honor your father and your mother.
He who speaks evil of father or mother, let him surely die."

27.36

But you say, "Let a man tell his father or his mother
'What you would have gained from me is given to God,'"
and no longer permit him to do anything for his father or
mother, thus making void the word of God through your
tradition that you hand on. And many such things do you do.

27.37

Well did Isaiah prophesy of you hypocrites, "This people
honors me with their lips, but their heart is far from me.
In vain do they worship me, teaching as doctrines
the precepts of men." You leave the commandment of God,
and hold fast to the tradition of men.

27.38

You justify yourselves before men,
but God knows your hearts. And what is highly esteemed
among men is an abomination in the sight of God.

27.39

It is written, "My house shall be called the house of prayer,
but you have made it a den of thieves."

27.40

Woe to you who are full now, for you shall hunger.
Woe to you who laugh now, for you shall mourn and weep.
Woe to you who are rich,
for you have received your consolation.

27.41

Woe to you when all men speak well of you,   27.42
for so did their fathers speak well of false prophets.

Woe to you lawyers! You load men with burdens   27.43
hard to bear, and you yourselves do not touch the burdens
with one of your fingers. You have taken away
the key of knowledge. You did not enter in yourselves,
and you hindered those who would enter.

Woe to you, Chorazin! Woe to you, Bethsaida!   27.44
If the evil works done in you had been done
in Tyre and Sidon, they would have repented long ago
in sackcloth and ashes. I say to you, it will be more tolerable
for Tyre and Sidon in the day of Judgment than for you.

And you, Capernaum, who are exalted to Heaven,   27.45
will be brought down to Hades. For if the evil works
done in you had not been done in Sodom, it would have
remained until this day. I say to you, it shall be more tolerable
for the land of Sodom in the day of Judgment than for you.

You are of your father, the devil, and your will   27.46
is to do your father's desires. He was a murderer
from the beginning, and has nothing to do with Truth
because there is no truth in him.

When he lies, he speaks according to his own nature,   27.47
for he is a liar and the father of lies.
But because I tell the truth, you do not believe me.
Which of you convicts me of sin?
If I tell the truth, why do you not believe me?

O you wretches. O you unfortunates.   27.48
O you pretenders to Truth. O you falsifiers of Knowledge.
O you sinners against the Spirit.

Can you still bear to listen, when it behooved you to speak 27.49
from the first? Can you still bear to sleep,
when it behooved you to be awake from the first,
so that the kingdom of Heaven might receive you?

It is easier for a pure one to fall into defilement,
and for a man of light to fall into darkness,
than for you to reign or not reign.

27.50

Had I been sent to those who listen to me, and had I spoken
with them, I would never have come down to earth.
So, then, be ashamed for these things.

27.51

You worship what you do not know.
We worship what we know.
But the hour is coming, and now is, when the true worshipers
will worship the Father in Spirit and Truth.
Such as these the Father seeks to worship him.

27.52

For God is Spirit and Truth, and those who worship him
must worship in Spirit and Truth.

27.53

I send the promise of the Father upon you. Wait in Jerusalem
until you are endued with power from on high.

27.54

For we are going to Jerusalem. There the Son of Man
will be betrayed to the priests and scribes,
and they will condemn him to death.

27.55

Therefore I must journey today, tomorrow,
and the day following. For it cannot be that a prophet
should perish outside of Jerusalem.

27.56

28. Dance of Praise

Hold hands in a circle around me 28.1
and answer *Amen* to my prayers.
Glory to thee, Father!
Glory to thee, Word!
Glory to thee, Grace!
Glory to thee, Spirit!
Glory to thee, Holy One!
Glory to thy Glory!
Amen.

We praise thee, O Father. 28.2
We give thanks to thee, O Light,
in whom darkness dwells not!

For what we give thanks, I say: 28.3
I would be saved, and I would save.
I would be loosed, and I would loose.
I would be wounded, and I would wound.
I would be pierced, and I would pierce.
I would be dissolved, and I would dissolve.
I would be consumed by love, and I would consume.
I would be begotten, and I would beget.
I would eat, and I would be eaten.
I would be washed, and I would wash.
I would understand, and I would be understood —
I would be all Understanding.
Amen!

Grace leads the dance. 28.4
I would play a pipe — dance ye all.
I would play a dirge — lament ye all.
The One dances with us.
The Twelfth Number above leads the dance.
All whose nature is to dance, dance.
Whoever dances not, knows not what is being done.
Amen!

I would flee, and I would stay.
I would be adorned, and I would adorn.
I would be atoned, and I would atone.
I have no dwelling, and I have dwellings.
I have no place, and I have places.
I have no temple, and I have temples.
I am a lamp to you who see me.
I am a mirror to you who understand me.
I am a door to you who knock at me.
I am a way to you who are a wayfarer.
Amen!

28.5

Now answer to my dancing!
See yourself in me who speaks.
And seeing what I do, keep silence on my mysteries.
Understand by dancing what I do.

28.6

For yours is the passion of man I am to suffer.
You could not at all be conscious of what you suffer,
were I not sent as your Word by the Father.
Seeing what I suffer, you saw me as suffering.
And seeing, you did not stand, but were moved wholly.
Moved to be wise.

28.7

You have me for a couch. Rest upon me.
Who I am you will know when I depart.
What now I am seen to be, that I am not.

28.8

What I am you shall see when you come.
If you knew how to suffer,
you would have the power not to suffer.
Know then how to suffer,
and you will have the power not to suffer.

28.9

That which you know not, I myself will teach you.
I am your God, not the Betrayer's.
I am kept in time with holy souls.
In me you will know the Word of wisdom.

28.10

Say them with me again:
Glory to thee, Father!
Glory to thee, Word!
Glory to thee, Holy Spirit!

But as for me, if you would know what I am,
I am the Word who did dance all things
and was not shamed at all.
It was I who leaped and danced.

Understand ye all, and understanding, say:
Glory to thee, Father!
Amen.

And now, go into the city. There you shall meet you a man
bearing a pitcher of water. Follow him, and where he goes
say to the good man of the house, "The Master asks,
'Where is the guest chamber? Where shall I eat the Passover
with my disciples?'" He will show you a large upper room,
furnished and prepared. There make ready for us.

29. Last Supper

My time has not yet come, but your time is always here. 29.1
What I am doing you do not know now,
but afterward you will understand.

Yet a little while I am with you, then I go to him who sent me. 29.2
You will seek me, but where I am going you cannot come.

The Son of Man will be betrayed into the hands of men. 29.3
He will suffer many things and be rejected
by the elders, priests and scribes. And he will be killed.
And on the third day he shall be raised again.

You will weep and lament, but the world will rejoice. 29.4
You will be full of sorrow, but your sorrow will turn into joy.

When a woman is in childbirth she has anguish because 29.5
her hour of travail has come. But when she is delivered
of the child, she no longer remembers the anguish,
such is her joy that a child is born into the world.

So it is that you will have sorrow now. 29.6
But I will see you again and your hearts will rejoice,
and no one shall take your joy from you.

And I will pray to the Father, and he will give you 29.7
another Counselor, to be with you forever —
the Spirit of Truth — whom the world cannot receive
because it neither sees him nor knows him.
Yet you know him, for he dwells with you, and in you.
I will not leave you desolate. I will come to you.

Yet a little while, and the world will see me no more. 29.8
But you will see me, and because I live, you will live also.
In that day you will know that I am in the Father,
and you are in me, and I am in you.

It is to your advantage that I go away. 29.9
If I do not go away, the Counselor will not come to you.
But if I go, I will send him to you.
And when he comes he will teach the world
concerning sin and righteousness and judgment.

Concerning sin, because they do not follow my Word. 29.10
Concerning righteousness, because I go to the Father
and you will see me no more. Concerning judgment,
because the ruler of this world is judged.

If you abide in me, and my Word abides in you, 29.11
ask whatever you will, and it shall be done for you.

By this my Father is glorified, that you bear much fruit, 29.12
and so prove to be my disciples.
As the Father loves me, so I love you. Abide in my love.

If you keep my Word you will abide in my love, 29.13
just as I have kept the Word of the Father and abide in his love.
These things I have spoken to you, that my joy may be in you,
and that your joy may be full.

Peace I leave you with. My peace I give to you. 29.14
Not as the world gives do I give to you.

Let not your hearts be troubled, neither let them be afraid. 29.15
You heard me say, "I go away, and I will come to you."
If you love me you will rejoice because I go to the Father
and the Father is greater than me.

And now I have told you before it takes place, so that when 29.16
it does take place, you may believe. I will no longer
talk much with you, for the ruler of this world is coming.
He has no power over me, but I do as the Father
has commanded, so that the world may know I love the Father.

Let not your hearts be troubled. 29.17
Believe in God, and believe also in me.
In my Father's house are many rooms. If it were not so,
would I have told you that I go to prepare a place for you?

And when I go and prepare a place for you, I will come again   29.18
and I will take you to myself, that where I am you may be also.

The hour is coming, indeed it has come,   29.19
when you will be scattered, every man to his home,
and will leave me alone. Yet I am not alone,
for the Father is with me.

I have said this to you that you may have peace in me.   29.20
In the world you have tribulation, but be of good cheer,
I have overcome the world that you may do likewise.

And now it is my fervent desire to eat this Passover with you   29.21
before I suffer. For I will no longer eat of it until I am fulfilled
in the kingdom of God.

Take this bread and eat of it.   29.22
This is my body that is given for you.
Do this in remembrance of me.

Take this cup and drink from it, all of you.   29.23
This is my blood of the new covenant,
which is shed for many for the forgiveness of sins.
I shall not drink again of the fruit of the vine
until I drink it new in the kingdom of God.

Truly I say to you, unless you eat the flesh of the Son of Man   29.24
and drink his blood, you have no life in you.
He who eats my flesh and drinks my blood has eternal Life,
and I will raise him up at the last day.

For my flesh is food indeed, and my blood is drink indeed.   29.25
He who eats my flesh and drinks my blood
abides in me, and I in him.

The living Father sent me. I live because of the Father.   29.26
He who eats my flesh will live because of me.
This is the bread of Heaven,
not the bread of your fathers who ate and died.
He who eats this bread will have eternal Life.

Yet behold, the hand of my betrayer is with me at this table.   29.27
It is one of the twelve, one who is dipping bread with me.
Truly, one of you shall betray me.

The Son of Man goes as it has been determined,   29.28
but woe to that man by whom he is betrayed.
It would be better for that man had he not been born.

I am not speaking of you all.   29.29
I know whom I have chosen, that the scripture be fulfilled:
"He who ate my bread has lifted his heel against me."
I tell you this now, before it takes place,
that when it does take place you may believe that I am he.

Then you will all fall away. For it is written,   29.30
"I will strike the shepherd and the sheep will be scattered."
Yet I will be raised up, and will go before you to Galilee.

All that the Father has is mine.   29.31
He will take what is mine and declare it to you.
A little while, and you will see me no more.
Again a little while, and you will see me.

You ask to be shown the secrets of Heaven, but I can reveal   29.32
nothing to you before I have put off this body of flesh.

You do not know what you ask.   29.33
Are you able to drink the cup I am about to drink,
and be baptized with the baptism I am baptized with?

If you are able, you will indeed drink my cup,   29.34
and be baptized with the baptism I am baptized with.
But to sit on my right hand and on my left is not mine to give.
It is for those for whom it is prepared by the Father.

If anyone serves me, he must follow my Way.   29.35
And where I am, there shall my servant be also.
If anyone serves me, the Father will honor him.

And now my soul is troubled, but what shall I say,   29.36
"Father, save me from this hour?"
Even so, my soul is exceeding sorrowful, even unto death.
Wait awhile here, my brothers, and watch with me.

The light is with you for a little longer.   29.37
Walk while you have the light, lest the darkness overtake you.
He who walks in darkness, knows not where he goes.

Are there not twelve hours in the day?   29.38
Whoever walks in the day does not stumble, because he sees
the light of this world. But whoever walks in the night,
stumbles, because the light is not in him.

Therefore, celebrate the remembrance of my death   29.39
at the Passover. Yet one of you who stands beside me
will be thrown into prison for my name's sake,
and he will be very grieved and sorrowful,
for while you celebrate the Passover,
he who is in custody knows he cannot celebrate it with you.

But I will send my power in the form of my angel,   29.40
and the door of the prison will open, and he will come out,
and come to you, to watch with you and to rest.

And when you complete my love and my remembrance   29.41
at the crowing of the cock, he will again be taken
and thrown into prison for a testimony,
until he comes out to preach as I have commanded you.
And you shall celebrate the drinking of the Passover
until I come from the Father with my wounds.

Hereafter you will see the Son of Man sitting at the   29.42
right hand of the Father, abiding in the realm of Heaven.

And now the hour is almost at hand.   29.43
The Son of Man shall be betrayed into the hands of sinners.
Let these words sink deep into your ears, for the Son of Man
is about to be delivered into the hands of men.

Greater love has no man than this,   29.44
that he lay down his life for his friends.

Sleep on now, brothers, and take your rest.   29.45

Abba, Father, all things are possible in you.   29.46
Let this cup pass from me.
Yet not what I will, but what thy will.

O Father, if this cup cannot pass away from me   29.47
unless I drink it, thy will be done.

Arise now, brothers. Let us be going.   29.48
He is at hand that doth betray me.
Arise, and do not be afraid.

30. Crucifixion

Judas, are you betraying the Son of Man with a kiss? 30.1

And you, have you come out as against a robber, 30.2
with swords and clubs to capture me?
Day after day I was with you in the temple teaching
and you did not seize me. But let the scriptures be fulfilled.

Put your sword into its sheath, Peter, 30.3
for all who take the sword will perish by the sword.
Shall I not drink the cup that the Father has given me?

I have spoken openly to the world. 30.4
I have always taught in synagogues and in the temple,
where all Jews come together. I have said nothing secretly.

He who speaks on his own authority seeks his own glory. 30.5
But he who seeks only the glory of God who sent him is true,
and in him there is no falsehood.

Did not Moses give you the law? Yet none of you 30.6
keeps the law. Why do you seek to kill me?

I tell you and you do not believe. 30.7
The works that I do in my Father's name bear witness to me,
yet you do not believe because you do not belong to my flock.

You do not realize who I am from what I say to you. 30.8
You have become like the Jews, who either love the tree
and hate its fruit, or love the fruit and hate the tree.

You would have no power over me 30.9
unless it had been given you from above.
He who delivered me to you has the greater sin.

You say that I am a king. I say, 30.10
for this I was born and for this I have come into the world:
to bear witness to Truth.
Everyone who is of Truth hears my voice.

My kingship is not of this world.   30.11
If my kingship were of this world my brethren would fight,
that I might not be handed over to the Jews.
But my kingship is not of the world.

It is for the people in Jerusalem I am being crucified,   30.12
and pierced with lances and reeds,
and given vinegar and gall to drink.

It is to you I am speaking. Listen to what I say.   30.13
I put into your mind to come up to this mountain
so that you may hear what a disciple should learn
from his teacher and a man of God.

These are the things that I would tell you so far.   30.14
Yet now I shall ascend to the place from whence I came.
But you, when I was eager to go, have cast me out.
Instead of accompanying me, you have pursued me.

Pay heed now to the glory that awaits me. Open your heart   30.15
and listen to the hymns that await me in Heaven.
For today I take my place at the right hand of the Father.

Do not hold me, for I have not yet ascended to the Father.   30.16
Go to my brethren and tell them I am ascending to my Father,
and your Father, to my God and your God.

I remember your tears and mourning and anguish.   30.17
They are far behind us. But now, you who are outside
the Father's inheritance, weep where it is necessary,
and mourn and preach what is good.
The Son is ascending as he must.

Father, the hour has come.   30.18
Glorify the Son that the Son may glorify you,
since you have given him power over all flesh,
to give eternal Life to all whom you have given him.

And this is eternal Life, that they know you, the One, God,   30.19
and Jesus Christ whom you have sent.

I glorified you on earth, having accomplished the work   30.20
you gave me to do. Now, Father, glorify me in your presence
with the glory I had with you before the world was made.

I have manifested your name to the men   30.21
you gave me out of the world. They were yours
and you gave them to me, and they have kept your Word.

They know that everything I gave them is from you,   30.22
for I have given them the Word you gave me,
and they have received it, and know I came from you,
and they believe that you did send me.

I am praying for them. I am not praying for the world,   30.23
but for those you have given me, for they are yours.
All mine are yours, and all yours are mine,
and I am glorified in them.

Now I am no more in the world, but they are in the world,   30.24
and I am coming to you. Holy Father, keep them
in your name, that they may be One, even as we are One.

While I was with them, I kept them in your name.   30.25
I have guarded them, and none of them is lost—
save the son of perdition, so that the scripture be fulfilled.
Now I am coming to you. And these things I speak
in the world, that they may have my joy fulfilled in themselves.

I have given them your Word, and the world has hated them   30.26
because they are not of the world, even as I am not of the world.
I do not pray that you take them out of the world,
but that you keep them from the evil one.
They are not of the world, even as I am not of the world.

Sanctify them in Truth. Your Word is Truth.   30.27
As you did send me into the world, so I have sent them
into the world. And for their sake I consecrate myself,
that they also may be consecrated in Truth.

I do not pray for these only, but also for those   30.28
who believe in me through their word, that they may all be One,
even as you, Father, are in me and me in you,
that they also may be in us, so that the world
may know that I am from you.

The glory you have given me I have given to them,   30.29
that they may be One, even as we are One,
I in them and you in me, that they may become perfectly One,
so that the world may know that you have sent me,
and have loved them even as you have loved me.

Father, I desire also that those you have given me   30.30
may be with me where I am, to behold the glory
you have given me before the beginning of the world,
because of your love for me.

Father, the world does not know you, but I know you,   30.31
and these know that you have sent me. I made known to them
your name, and I will make it known that the love
with which you love me is in them, as I am in them.

Woman, behold your son. Brother, behold your mother.   30.32

Father, forgive them, for they know not what they do.   30.33

Truly I say to you, today you will be with me in Paradise.   30.34

I thirst.   30.35

My God, my God, why have you forsaken me?   30.36

It is complete.   30.37

Father, into your hands I commit my spirit.   30.38

31. Resurrection

There comes a time and an hour when what comes next   31.1
is to go to the Father.

For this reason have I perfected all mercy.   31.2
Without being begotten I was born of man.
Without having flesh I put on flesh and grew up,
that I might regenerate you who were begotten in the flesh,
and in regeneration you obtain the resurrection in your flesh,
a garment that will not pass away.

For all who hope and believe in him who sent me,   31.3
the Father has found pleasure in you, and to whomever I will,
I give the hope of the Kingdom.

As the Father awakened me from the dead,   31.4
in the same manner you also will arise in the flesh,
and he will cause you to rise up above the heavens
to the place I have spoken to you of from the beginning,
which he who sent me has prepared for you.

The flesh of every man will rise,   31.5
with his soul alive, and his spirit.

I have suffered none of those things they will say of me.   31.6
Even the suffering I showed to you in my dance,
I will that it be called a mystery.

What you are, that I have shown you.   31.7
But what I am is known to me alone, and no one else.
Let me have what is mine.

What is yours you must see through me.   31.8
But me you must see truly — not that which I am,
but that which you, as my brothers, are able to know.

You hear that I suffered yet I suffered not.   31.9
You hear that I suffered not, yet I did suffer.

You hear that I was pierced, yet I was not wounded,   31.10
that I was hanged, yet I was not hanged,
that blood flowed from me, yet blood did not flow.
In a word, what they say of me I did not endure.
But what they do not say, those things I did suffer.

What these are, I now secretly show you,   31.11
for I know that you will understand.
You must know me then, as the torment of the Logos,
the piercing of the Logos, the blood of the Logos,
the wounding of the Logos, the fastening of the Logos,
the death of the Logos.

And so I speak, discarding the body of man.   31.12
The first that you must know is the Logos,
then you must know the Lord, then thirdly
know the man and what he suffered.

I took my place in the midst of the world, and I appeared   31.13
to them in flesh. I found all of them intoxicated.
I found none of them thirsty.

And my soul became afflicted for the sons of men,   31.14
because they are blind in their hearts and do not have sight.

For empty they came into the world,   31.15
and empty they will leave the world.
But for the moment they are intoxicated.
When they shake off their wine, then they will repent.

O foolish ones, and slow of heart to believe   31.16
in all that the prophets have spoken! Ought not the Christ
to have suffered these things and entered into Glory?

Why are you troubled? Why do doubts arise in your hearts?   31.17
Behold my hands and my feet, that it is I myself.
Touch me and see, for a spirit does not have flesh and bones
as you see I have. Be of good cheer! It is I. Do not be afraid.

It is written that it was necessary for the Christ to suffer   31.18
and to rise from the dead on the third day, and that repentance
and remission of sins should be preached in his name
to all nations, beginning at Jerusalem.
And you are witnesses of these things.

I told you this while I was still with you, that all things   31.19
must be fulfilled that are written in the law of Moses
and the prophets and the psalms concerning me.

For whom are you weeping? Do not weep.   31.20
I am he whom you seek. Go to your brothers and say to them,
"Come, our master has risen from the dead."

He whom you see on the tree glad and laughing   31.21
is the living Jesus. This one into whose hands and feet
they drive the nails is his fleshly part,
which is the substitute being put to shame,
the one who came into being in his likeness.
But look at him and me.

He who stands with him is the living Christ,   31.22
the first in him, whom they seized and released,
who stands joyfully looking at those who did him violence,
while they are divided among themselves. He laughs
at their lack of perception, knowing they are born blind.

Come, and do not be afraid. I am your teacher,   31.23
whom you, Peter, denied three times before the cock crowed.
Do you now deny again? Why do you doubt?
Why do you not believe? I am he who spoke to you
concerning my flesh, my death, and my resurrection.

That you may know it is me, touch my hand, Peter,   31.24
and the nail wound in my palm. And you, Thomas,
the wound in my side. And you, Andrew,
see whether my foot leaves a footprint. For it is written,
"A ghost or demon leaves no print on the ground."

But you cannot have a hem of my garment,   31.25
for it is not the garment I wore before I was crucified.

I put on the garment of flesh, in which I was born and died,   31.26
and was buried and rose again through the Father,
that it might be fulfilled what was said by the prophet David
concerning my death and resurrection:

"Lord, how numerous they have become who oppress me.   31.27
Many have risen up against me. Many say to my soul,
'He has received no salvation by his God.'
But you, O Lord, are my refuge, my glory,
and he who lifts up my head."

When the Counselor comes, whom I shall send to you   31.28
from the Father — the Spirit of Truth who proceeds
from the Father — he will bear witness to me.
And you also are witnesses,
because you have been with me from the beginning.

Wait for me in this place, for today a sacrifice is offered   31.29
in paradise, that I may receive it after my arrival.
The souls of the righteous, when they leave the body,
go to paradise, and unless I am present they cannot enter.
Even when I taught among you, I sat at the right hand
of the Father and received these sacrifices in paradise.

In this age, thirty thousand souls leave the world each day,   31.30
and of these only three are admitted to paradise.
The number of souls born into the world each day
is only one over and above those who leave the world.

What is your merit if you do the will of the Father   31.31
and it is not given to you from him as a gift
while you are tempted by Satan?

But if you are oppressed by Satan, and persecuted,   31.32
and yet you do the Father's will, I say that he will love you,
and make you equal with me, and reckon you to have
become beloved through his providence by your own choice.

So will you not cease loving the flesh and being afraid   31.33
of sufferings? Or do you not know that you have yet to be
abused, and to be accused unjustly, and have yet to be shut up
in prison, and condemned unlawfully, and crucified
without reason, and buried shamefully, as was I myself,
by the evil one? Do you dare to spare the flesh,
you for whom the Spirit is an encircling wall?

If you consider how long the world existed before you,   31.34
and how long it will exist after you,
you will find that your life is but one single day,
and your sufferings one single hour.

For the Good will not enter into the world.   31.35
Scorn death, therefore, and take thought for Life!
Remember my cross and my death, and you will live!

None will be saved unless they take up my cross.   31.36
But those who take up my cross, theirs is the kingdom of God.

Therefore become seekers for death,   31.37
like the dead who seek for life.
For that which they seek is revealed to them.
And what is there to trouble them?

As for you, when you examine death, it will teach you purpose.   31.38
None of those who fear death will be saved,
for the kingdom of death belongs to those
who put themselves to death.

Become better than me. Become sons of the Holy Spirit!   31.39

Whoever keeps my Word and follows my Way   31.40
will be a son of the Light, a son of God the Father.
It is for the sake of those who keep and do my Word
that I have come from Heaven.

I, the Word, became flesh and died, teaching and guiding,   31.41
that some shall be saved, but the others eternally ruined—
being punished by fire in flesh and spirit.

If you are truly troubled on account of these, you do well.   31.42
For so are the righteous anxious about the sinners,
and they pray and implore God and ask his mercy.
And if the righteous entreat me concerning the plight
of sinners, I will hear their requests.

Now I go to the place from whence I came.   31.43
If you wish to come with me, come.

Chapter VI
Prophesy

War and Tribulation
Apocalypse
Judgment
Hell and Damnation
The Seven Churches

It could be fairly said that taken as a whole the sayings attributed to Jesus expound a "carrot and stick" theology, offering the carrot of eternal Life in the kingdom of God if you follow his Way, and the stick of eternal pain and torture if you don't. The sermons in Part VI include sayings that expound at length on the stick.

"War and Tribulation" and "Apocalypse" focus on what will happen to the physical world and those in it if we don't repent, while "Judgment" outlines the selection process for our personal eternal assignments. "Hell and Damnation" expounds in detail on what happens to us if we don't make the cut, and catalogs so many ways to sin ourselves into Hell there seems almost no way to avoid it. "The Seven Churches" contains the words attributed to Christ in the Book of Revelation.

The sayings found in these sermons comprise an aspect of Jesus' teachings that many of us find difficult to reconcile with the Jesus of love, forgiveness and enlightenment. Yet, if we envision the wide variety of people he no doubt encountered, and remember how confrontational he could be, we might imagine that when Jesus found himself among deeply ignorant people, he would know their best hope of taking the next step towards salvation was to, quite literally, have the fear of God put in them.

32. War and Tribulation

There are those who say to me, "Blessed is the womb   32.1
that bore you and the breasts that nourished you."
But I say to you, "Blessed are those who have received
the Word of the Father and truly kept it."

For there will be days when you will say,   32.2
"Blessed are the wombs that have not conceived,
and the breasts that have not given milk."

Men think, perhaps, it is peace I have come to cast   32.3
upon the world. They do not know it is dissension
I have come to cast upon the world — fire, sword, and war.

Where there are five in a house, three will be against two,   32.4
and two against three, Father against son,
and son against the father. And they will each stand alone.

I come to cast fire upon the world,   32.5
and how I wish it were already blazing!

Do not think that I come to bring peace on earth.   32.6
I come not to bring peace but a sword.
I come to "set a man against his father,
a daughter against her mother, and a daughter-in-law
against her mother-in-law," and so it will be that
"a man's enemies will be those of his own household."

For he who loves father or mother more than me   32.7
is not worthy of me. And he who loves son or daughter
more than me is not worthy of me. And he who does not
take up his cross and follow my Way is not worthy of me.

For he who holds his life will lose it,   32.8
but he who leaves his life for my sake, will find eternal Life.

He who is near to me is near the fire.   32.9
He who is far from me, is far from the Kingdom.

Therefore, now, he who has a money bag let him take it,   32.10
and likewise a knapsack. And he who has no sword,
let him sell his garment and buy one.

For that which is written must still be accomplished in me: 32.11
"He was numbered with the transgressors."
For the things concerning me have an end.

You shall hear of wars and rumors of wars.   32.12
Do not be troubled. For all these things must come to pass.
But the end is not yet.

For nation shall rise against nation and kingdom   32.13
against kingdom, and there shall be famine, and pestilence,
and earthquakes in many places.
And there will be fearful sights and great signs from heaven.
Yet these are just the birth pangs of sorrow and tribulation.

When you see Jerusalem surrounded by armies,   32.14
know that its desolation is near. When you see
the abomination of desolation spoken of by Daniel,
stand in the holy place. When you see the desolating sacrilege
set up where it ought not to be, let all in Judea
flee to the mountains.

Let him who is on his housetop not come down to gather   32.15
his belongings. Let him who is in the field
not return to gather his clothes. Remember Lot's wife.

Let those in the cities depart, and let not those   32.16
in the countryside enter. For these are the days of vengeance,
in which all things written are fulfilled.

Do you see these great buildings?   32.17
In the days to come not one stone will remain upon another.
Everything shall be thrown down.

And woe to those who are with child in these days,   32.18
and to those who suckle their young.
And pray your flight be not in winter, nor on the Sabbath.

For in these days there will be tribulation unlike any
ever witnessed from the beginning of Creation until now.
And never again will there be such tribulation as this.

32.19

There will be great distress in the land, and great wrath
turned loose upon this people. They will die by the sword
and be taken as slaves by all nations. Gentiles will trample
Jerusalem, until their time also is fulfilled.

32.20

And if the Lord does not shorten the days, no flesh shall be
saved. Yet for his chosen elect, he shall shorten the days.

32.21

In those years and days there shall be war upon war.
The four corners of the world will be shaken and will fight
against each other. There will be a great disturbance
of the clouds, and darkness, and drought, and persecution
of the elect who follow my Way.
Dissension and conflict and evil action shall reign.

32.22

Among them will be some who say they believe in me,
yet commit evil and teach vain teachings. Others
will follow them, and submit themselves to their riches,
their depravity, their mania for drinking and gifts of bribery.
They will be ruled by a vain hierarchy of persons
who demand their esteem.

32.23

For as it was in the days of Noah,
so shall it be with the coming of the Son of Man.
In the days before the flood they were eating and drinking,
marrying and giving in marriage. They knew nothing
of the flood until the day Noah entered the ark.
And the flood came. And they were all destroyed.

32.24

Likewise it was in the days of Lot.
The Sodomites ate and drank, bought and sold,
planted and built. Then on the day Lot left Sodom,
the heavens rained fire and brimstone and destroyed it all.
So shall it be when the Son of Man appears.

32.25

In that day, where there are two in bed, one will be taken   32.26
and the other one left. Where two women are grinding
at the mill, one will be taken and the other one left.
Where two men are working in a field,
one will be taken and the other one left.

Brother will deliver up brother to death,   32.27
and the father will deliver up his child, and children
will rise against parents and have them put to death.
Iniquity will abound and the love of many will wax cold.
You will be hated by all because of me.
But he who endures to the end will be saved.

And in the days after that tribulation, the sun will go dark   32.28
and the moon will not give its light. The stars will fall,
and the powers in the heavens will be shaken.

Then shall appear the sign of the Son of Man.   32.29
And the tribes of the earth shall mourn.
And the tribes of the earth shall see the Son of Man
appear in the clouds of heaven with great power
and great glory. And the Son of Man will send out angels
to gather his elect from the four winds,
and from the far reaches of heaven and earth.

But woe to those who see the Son of Man.   32.30
Blessed are they who do not see him,
who do not associate with him, who do not speak with him,
who do not hear anything from him. Yours is Life!
He has healed you of your illness, that you might reign.

And woe to those who find relief from their illness,   32.31
yet relapse into illness. Blessed are they
who have not been ill, who know relief before falling ill.
Yours is the kingdom of God.

Therefore I say to you, become full and leave no space   32.32
within you empty, for he who is coming can mock you.

If you knew — you, now, in this your day —   32.33
the things that make for your peace!
But they are hidden from your eyes.

Days will come upon you when your enemies   32.34
will build an embankment around you, and surround you,
and close you in on every side, and level you
and your children within you to the ground.
And they will not leave in you one stone upon another,
because you did not know the time of your visitation.

If the master of the house had known what hour the thief   32.35
would come, he would have watched and not allowed
his house to be broken into. Therefore you also be ready.
For the Son of Man is coming at an hour you do not expect.

Watch therefore, and pray always, that you may be counted   32.36
worthy to escape all these things that will come to pass,
and to stand before the Son of Man.

Look at the fig tree, and all the trees.   32.37
When they are budding, you know that summer is near.
Likewise, when you see all these things happening,
know that the kingdom of God is near.

Truly, this generation will by no means pass away until   32.38
all these things take place. Heaven and earth will pass away,
but my words will by no means pass away.

33. Apocalypse

Listen well, for I am the son of God the Father,   33.1
and I am the father of all spirits.
Hear from me the signs that will signify
the end of this world, and how the end of this world
will come to pass before my elect go forth from the world.

I now tell you openly what will happen to men.   33.2
When these things are to take place, even the princes
of the angels do not know, for they are hidden from them.

The kings will divide the world among themselves, and there   33.3
will be hunger and pestilence and much distress on earth.
The sons of men will perish by the sword and be enslaved
in all nations, and everywhere there will be grave disorder.

There will be signs in the sun and the moon and the stars.   33.4
On earth, disaster and confusion will reign.
Seas will roar with storms and towering waves.
Men's hearts will fail from fear of what is to come,
and the powers of the heavens will be shaken.

When the hour of the end draws near   33.5
there will be great signs in the sky for seven days,
and the powers of the heavens will be set in motion.

At the third hour of the first day a mighty voice will sound   33.6
In the firmament. A cloud of blood will rise up from the north
and there will follow great rolls of thunder and flashes
of fierce lightning, and it will cover the whole of the heavens.

Then blood will rain on all the earth.   33.7
These are the signs of the first day.

On the second day a great voice will sound in the firmament   33.8
and the earth will be moved from its place. The heavens
will open in the east, and the smoke of a great fire
will burst forth and cover the whole of the firmament,
from the east to the end of the west.

And there will be great fear and terror in the world.   33.9
These are the signs of the second day.

On the third day, at the third hour, there will be a great voice   33.10
in the heavens, and the depths of the earth will roar out
from the four corners of the world. The zenith of heaven
will be laid open, and the air will be filled with pillars of smoke.
The evil stench of sulfur will last until the tenth hour.

Men will say, "The end is upon us and we shall perish!"   33.11
These are the signs of the third day.

At the first hour of the fourth day,   33.12
the Abyss will melt and rumble from the land of the east.
Then the whole earth will be shaken by the force
of an earthquake beyond imagination.

In that day the idols of the heathen will fall,   33.13
as will all the buildings on earth.
These are the signs of the fourth day.

On the fifth day, at the sixth hour, there will be great thunder   33.14
in the heavens, and the powers of the light will flash,
and the sphere of the sun will burst, and great darkness
will be on the whole world as far as the west.

The air will be sorrowful without sun and moon,   33.15
and the stars will cease their work.
All men will see as if they were enclosed in a sack,
and they will despise the life of this world.
These are the signs of the fifth day.

At the fourth hour of the sixth day there will be a great voice   33.16
in the heavens. The firmament will be split from east to west,
and through the rents in the heavens the angels
will look out on the earth. And everyone on earth
will see angels looking out on them from heaven.

And they will flee into the tombs,
and hide themselves from the righteous angels, saying,
"Oh, that the earth would open up and swallow us."
For such things will happen as never have happened
since this world was created.

33.17

Then they will see me come in the light of the Father,
with the power and glory of all the holy angels.
And on my arrival the fire of paradise will be loosed,
for paradise is enclosed with fire — the eternal fire that devours
the earth and all the elements of the world.

33.18

Then the spirits and souls of the saints
will come forth from paradise and go into the world.
And each will go to where its body is laid up and say,
"Here my own body is laid up."

33.19

And when the voice of those great spirits is heard
there will be an earthquake over all the earth,
and the force of the earthquake will shatter
all the mountains above and all the rocks beneath.

33.20

Then each spirit will return to its own vessel,
and the bodies of the saints who sleep will rise.
Their bodies will be changed
into the image and likeness and honor of the holy angels,
and into the power of the image of the holy Father.

33.21

Then they will put on the garment of eternal Life,
the garment from the cloud of Light,
which has never been seen in this world.
For this Light comes from the kingdom of Heaven
by the power of the Father, and it will wrap with its glory
every spirit who follows my Way.

33.22

Then they will be clothed by the hands of the holy angels,
and carried off in a cloud of light into the ether.
And rejoicing, they shall join me in Heaven,
and abide in the Light of the Father.

33.23

There will be great joy for them in the presence   33.24
of their Father and the holy angels.
These are the signs of the sixth day.

At the eighth hour of the seventh day,   33.25
there will be voices in the four corners of the heavens.
The firmament will be filled with holy angels,
and they will argue among themselves all day.

In that day the elect will be saved by the holy angels   33.26
from the destruction of the world, and those not among
the elect will know that the hour of their destruction is near.
These are the signs of the seventh day.

And when the seven days are finished, on the eighth day   33.27
at the sixth hour, there will be a gentle and pleasant voice
in the firmament of the east, and the angel who has power
over all the angels will be made manifest.

And there will go forth with him all the holy angels,   33.28
riding the holy Father's chariots of clouds, rejoicing,
and flying in the air under heaven to deliver the elect
who have followed my Way. And they will rejoice
that the destruction of the world has come.

I tell you what will happen so that not only you,   33.29
but those you will teach and who henceforth follow my Way,
shall know. There are many who will hear these men,
and who will follow my Way because of them.

For in those years and in those days this will happen.   33.30
The believers and unbelievers alike will see a trumpet
in the heavens. Great stars shall be visible in daylight.
A dragon will stretch across heaven and earth.
Burning stars shall fall as great hailstones of terrible fire.

And the sun and moon will fight against each other,   33.31
and there will be thunder and lightning and earthquakes.
Cities will fall to the ground and men will die in their ruins.

There will be constant drought, and a great plague   33.32
across the land causing death so extensive and quick
that those who die will lack a grave.

Children and parents will lay dying in one bed,   33.33
And the parent will not turn to his child, nor the child
to his parent. Nor will a neighbor turn to his neighbor.

Then those who are forsaken will rise up and see those   33.34
who forsook them when they brought on the plague.
And they will be gripped by hatred and jealousy,
and they will take for themselves from the other.
Yet what is to follow will be even worse.

There are those who shall not die from the torment of plague.   33.35
And if they suffer torment, such suffering
will be a test for them, whether they have faith,
and keep my Word, and follow my Way.

And they will rise up after only a few days   33.36
so that God may be glorified, and I with him.
For it is he who sends me to you.

I tell you this, and you shall tell it to Israel and the Gentiles.   33.37
They also can be saved, and follow my Way, and escape
the distress of the plague, and what is to follow.
For those who escape death from the plague
will be thrown into prison and tortured like thieves.

And the gospel of the Kingdom will be preached   33.38
in all the world for a witness unto all nations.
Then the end will come.

34. Judgment

Which falls away, flesh or spirit?   34.1
Flesh falls away.

What has fallen will arise and what is ill will be made sound,   34.2
that the Father may therein be praised.
As he has given me, so I give to you and to all who receive me.

Your soul gives birth to your flesh so that you might work   34.3
and be judged by your works — whether good or bad — in order
to become an elect and an example for all who follow my Way,
and so that you might live the Truth of the Father.

Then shall the righteous Judgment take place,   34.4
for the Father wills it. He has told me,
"On the day of the Judgment do not favor the rich nor spare
the poor, but deliver to each the consequences of his sins."

Yet to those who have loved me,   34.5
and to those who now love me and keep my Word,
I shall grant rest, and Life in the kingdom
of the Father in Heaven.

This is the Judgment, that the Light is come into the world.   34.6
Yet men love darkness rather than light
because their deeds are evil.
For everyone who does evil hates the light,
and does not come to the light, lest his deeds be exposed.

But he who does what is true comes into the light,   34.7
that it may be clearly seen that his deeds
have been wrought in God.

The Father will become angry at the wickedness of men.   34.8
For their offenses are many
and the horror of their impurity corrupts their lives.

What is allotted to those who have faith in my Word?   34.9
Truly, as David prophesized about me and my disciples,
so it will be also for all who follow my Way.
How long will you remain slow of heart?

But there will also be in the world, deceivers and enemies   34.10
of righteousness, and they will fulfill the prophecy of David,
who said: "They are quick to shed blood and their tongues
weave deceit. The venom of serpents is on their lips.
I see you wandering with a thief and taking your share
with a fornicator. Even now as you sit, you slander
your brother and set a trap for your mother's son.
Do you think I should be like you?"

The prophet of God has spoken about everything,   34.11
so that all may be fulfilled as it was spoken.

How will the Judgment of righteousness take place   34.12
for the sinners and the righteous?

When the Son of Man comes in his glory, and all the holy angels   34.13
with him, he shall sit upon the throne of his glory.
And before him shall be gathered all souls.
And he shall separate them one from another, as a shepherd
divides his sheep from the goats. And he shall set the sheep
on his right hand, and the goats he shall set on his left.

And he will say to those on his right, "You are the blessed   34.14
of the Father. You shall inherit the Kingdom
prepared for you from the foundation of the world.

For I was hungry and you gave me food. I was thirsty   34.15
and you gave me drink. I was a stranger and you took me in.
I was naked and you clothed me. I was sick and you visited me.
I was in prison and you came to me."

And the righteous will question him, saying, "Lord,   34.16
when did we see you hungry and feed you, or see you thirsty
and give you drink? When did we see you a stranger
and take you in, or see you naked and give you clothes?
When did we see you sick or in prison and come to you?"

And the Son of Man will answer, saying,   34.17
"Insomuch as you have done it for the least of these,
my brethren, you have done it for me."

Then shall the Son of Man say to them on his left,   34.18
"Depart from me. You are cursed into the everlasting fire
prepared for you by Satan and his angels.

For I was hungry and you gave me no food. I was thirsty   34.19
and you gave me no drink. I was a stranger and you did not
take me in. I was naked and you clothed me not.
I was sick and you did not visit me.
I was in prison and you did not come to me."

And these shall also question him, saying,   34.20
"Lord, when did we see you hungry and not feed you,
or thirsty and not give you drink?
When did we see you a stranger and not take you in,
or naked and not give you clothes?
When did we see you sick or in prison and not come to you?"

And the Son of Man shall answer, saying,   34.21
"Insomuch as you have done it not for the least of these,
my brethren, you have done it not for me."

And as the righteous enter eternal Life in Heaven,   34.22
these descend into everlasting pain.

For the serpent taught them to eat of wickedness,   34.23
begetting, lust, and destruction,
that they might be useful to him.

Where will the souls of these go when they come out   34.24
of their flesh? The soul in which the power of God becomes
superior to the despicable spirit is strong, and flees from evil.

Hear now what they shall experience in the last days,   34.25
when the day of the Judgment of God comes.

On the day of the Judgment of God,
all the children of men—from the east unto the west—
will be gathered before the eternal Father.
He will command Hell to open its iron bars
and give up all that it holds.

And he will command the beasts and fowls
to give back all the flesh they have devoured,
for he desires that men should appear again.
With God nothing perishes and nothing is impossible,
for everything is in him.

With the word of God all things shall come to pass
on the day of Judgment, just as all things came to pass
when he created the world with his Word.
He commanded and it was done. So shall it be
in the last days, for everything is possible with God.

God says in the scriptures: "Son of Man, prophesy
upon the many bones and command the bones to life—
bone unto bone in joints, and thereupon sinews,
nerves, flesh, skin, and hair."

The great Uriel shall give soul and spirit to these bones
according to the will of God, for God has given him authority
on the day of Judgment over the resurrection of the dead.

As there are those who fulfill what is good,
so do the wicked manifest. All shall be judged righteously
according to their works and actions,
and the wicked shall be delivered to ruin.

These things shall come to pass in the day of Judgment to
those who have fallen from faith in God and committed sin:

Cataracts of fire shall be let loose, and obscurity and darkness
shall cover and veil the entire world.
The waters shall be transformed into coals of fire,
and all that is in them shall burn, and the sea shall become fire.
Under all the heavens there shall be a fierce fire that cannot
be put out, and which flows for the judgment of wrath.

The stars will be melted by fire as if they had not been created,   34.34
and the fastnesses of heaven shall pass away for want of water,
and become as though they had not been created.

And the lightnings of heaven shall be no more,   34.35
and by their enchantment, they shall alarm the world.
And the spirits of dead bodies shall be like to them,
and at the command of God will become fire.

And as the whole of creation is dissolved, those in the east   34.36
shall flee to the west and those in the west shall flee to the east.
Those in the south shall flee to the north and those in the north
shall flee to the south. But everywhere
the wrath of fearful fire shall overtake them.

And an unquenchable flame shall drive them,   34.37
and bring them to the judgment of wrath in the stream
of unquenchable fire that flows, flaming with fire.

And when its waves separate one from another, seething,   34.38
there shall be gnashing of teeth among the children of men.

In the regeneration, when the Son of Man sits on the throne   34.39
of his glory, you who have followed my Way will also sit
on twelve thrones, judging the twelve tribes of Israel.

Everyone who has left houses or brothers or sisters   34.40
or father or mother or wife or children or lands
for the sake of righteousness,
shall receive a hundredfold, and inherit eternal Life.
Many who are first will be last, and the last first.

Strive to enter through the narrow gate,   34.41
for many will seek to enter and will not be able.
When the master of the house has shut the door
and you stand outside and knock, saying,
"Lord, Lord, open for us," he will answer, saying,
"I do not know you," or "Where are you from?"

And you will say, "We ate and drank in your presence,   34.42
and you taught in our streets." But he will say,
"I tell you I do not know you. Where you are from?
Depart from me, all you workers of iniquity."

There will be weeping and gnashing of teeth   34.43
when you see Abraham, Isaac, and Jacob and all the prophets
in the kingdom of God, and yourselves thrust out.

They will come from the east and the west, from the north   34.44
and the south, and sit down in the kingdom of God.
And there are last who will be first, and first who will be last.

Not everyone who says to me, "Lord, Lord,"   34.45
shall enter the kingdom of Heaven.
Only he who does the will of the Father.

Many will say to me in that day, "Lord, Lord,   34.46
have we not prophesied in your name, cast out demons
in your name, and done many wonders in your name?"
And I will say to them, "I never knew you.
Depart from me, you who practice lawlessness!"

Though you should be joined to me in my bosom,   34.47
if you do not keep my Word, I will cast you out and say to you:
"Depart from me. I know you not, you doers of evil."
So will I speak to those who go into destruction.

Why do you say of sinners, "To not have been created   34.48
would be better for them"? You doubt God.
You cannot have more compassion than God for his images,
for he has created them. He has brought them forth
from when they were not.

Because you know the lamentation that sinners   34.49
shall encounter in the last days, your heart is saddened.
But I tell you the ways in which they sin against the Most High.

For he who rejects me and does not receive my teachings   34.50
has a judge. On the last day,
the Word that I have spoken will be his judge.

But to you I have given that you should be children   34.51
of the light in God, and should be pure from all wickedness
and from all power of the Judgment.

And to those who believe in me through you,   34.52
I will do the same. As I have said and promised you,
they shall be set free of prison and rescued from the chains
and the spears, and the terrible fire.

God will send his angels with the sound of a great trumpet.   34.53
And his angels will gather together his elect
from the four winds, from one end of the heavens to the other.

But of that day and hour no one knows. Not even the angels   34.54
of Heaven know, nor even does the Son know.
Only the Father knows. Take heed, therefore, and watch.
You do not know that day and hour.

Watch, for you do not know   34.55
when the master of the house will come.
He may come at evening, at midnight, at cockcrow or morn.
Watch, lest he come suddenly and find you asleep.
Truly I say to you: Watch!

Watch, for you know not the hour the Lord will come.   34.56
If the good man of the house had known
what hour the thief would come, he would have watched,
and would not have suffered his house to be broken up.

Behold, I come as a thief.   34.57
Blessed is he who watches and keeps his garments,
lest he walk naked, and they see his shame.

If the owner of a house knows a thief is coming,   34.58
he will begin his vigil before he comes,
not let him ransack his house and carry off his goods.

You then, be on your guard against the world. Arm yourself   34.59
with great strength lest the thieves find a way to come at you.
For the difficulty you expect will surely materialize.

Fortunate is the man who knows where the brigands   34.60
will enter, so that he may get up, muster his domain,
and arm himself before they invade.

When a strong man, fully armed, guards his own palace,   34.61
his goods are in peace. But when one stronger than he
overcomes him, he takes from him all the arms
in which he trusted, and divides his spoils.

It is not possible for a thief to enter the house of a strong man   34.62
and take it by force, unless he binds the strong man's hands.
Then the thief can ransack his house.

Therefore, be ready. For in the hour you think the Son of Man   34.63
cometh not, the Son of Man shall come.

Take heed, lest your heart be weighed down with carousing,   34.64
drunkenness, and the cares of daily life.
For that day will come unexpectedly, and it will come
as a snare for all who live in the realm of the earth.

For every idle word men speak,   34.65
they will give account of it in the day of Judgment.
By your words you shall be justified, and by your words
you shall be condemned.

Now is the Judgment of this world.   34.66
Now shall the ruler of this world be cast out.

Why will the Judgment take place? That the wheat   34.67
may be put in its barn and the chaff thrown into the fire.

The kingdom of Heaven is like a dragnet cast into the sea,   34.68
which gathered some of every kind.
And when it was full the fishermen drew it to shore
and gathered the good into baskets, and threw the bad away.

So it will be at the end of the age.   34.69
The angels will come forth to gather the just into Heaven
and cast the wicked into the furnace of fire.
There will be wailing and gnashing of teeth.

You will see the Son of Man,
coming in great clouds of power and glory.
When these things begin to happen, look up.
Lift up your heads, for your salvation draws near.

34.70

The Son will come in the glory of the Father, with his angels,
and each of you shall be rewarded according to your works.

34.71

Truly, there are those among you who shall know the Son
and the Kingdom before they taste death.

34.72

To him that overcomes will I grant to sit at my right hand
on my throne, even as I have overcome,
and sit at the right hand of the Father on his throne,
for all ages, forever and ever. Amen.

34.73

35. Hell and Damnation

He who listens to the Word and turns away his face,   35.1
or sneers at it, or smirks at these things,
truly I tell you that he will be handed over to the Ruler above,
who rules over all the powers as their king,
and he will turn that one around
and cast him from Heaven down to the abyss,
and he will be imprisoned in a dark, narrow place.

And he will not be able to turn nor move   35.2
on account of the great depth of Tartars,
and the heavy bitterness of Hades that besets him.
Such as these are imprisoned so that they might not escape.
Their madness will not be forgiven.

And the Rulers, who will pursue you,   35.3
will deliver them to the angel Tartarouchos,
and he will pursue them with whips of fire and fiery scourges
that cast a shower of sparks into the face of the one pursued.

If he flees westward, he finds the fire. If he flees southward,   35.4
he finds it there as well. If he turns northward,
the threat of seething fire meets him again.

Nor does he find the way to the east so as to flee there   35.5
and be saved. He did not find it when he was in the body,
so he will not find it in the day of Judgment.

And all will see how I come upon an eternal shining cloud,   35.6
with the angels of God who will sit with me on the throne
of glory at the right hand of my Father in Heaven.

He will set a crown upon my head,   35.7
and when the nations see it, each nation will weep for itself.
And he shall command them to go into the river of fire,
while the deeds of each individual stand before him.

Recompense shall be given to each according to his work.   35.8
As for the elect who have done good,
they will come to me and will not see death by devouring fire.

But the evil creatures, the sinners and the hypocrites,   35.9
will stand in the depths of the darkness that passes not away,
and their punishment is the fire.

Angels shall bring forward their sins, and prepare for them   35.10
a place wherein they shall be punished forever,
each according to his offense.

Uriel, the angel of God, shall bring the souls of all the sinners   35.11
who perished in the flood, and of all who dwell in idols,
in every molten image, in every desire, in every painting,
and of all that dwell on all the hills, and in all the stones,
and by every wayside, whom men call gods.

And they shall be burned with them in eternal fire.   35.12
And after all of them, with their dwelling places,
have been destroyed, they will be punished eternally.

Then will men and women come to the place   35.13
prepared for them. By their tongues with which they
blasphemed the way of righteousness will they be hung up.
There is spread out for them unquenchable fire.

And behold another place — a great pit filled with those who   35.14
have denied righteousness. Angels of punishment visit them,
and here do kindle upon them the fire of their punishment.

And here two women are hung up by their necks,   35.15
and by their hair are cast into the pit.
These are they who plaited their hair, not to create beauty,
but to turn to fornication, that they might ensnare
the souls of men to destruction.

And the men who lay with them in fornication   35.16
are hung by their thighs in that burning place,
and they say to one another, "We did not know
that we would come into everlasting torture."

Murderers, and those who made common cause with them,   35.17
are cast into the fire in a place full of venomous beasts.
And they are tormented without rest as they feel their pains.
And their worms are as numerous as a dark cloud.

And the angel Ezrael will bring forth the souls   35.18
of those who have been murdered. And they will see
the torment of those who killed them, and will hear them say,
"Righteousness and justice is the judgment of God.
For we indeed heard, but did not believe, that we would come
to this place of eternal judgment."

And near this flame there is a great and very deep pit,   35.19
and into it flows all kind of evil things from everywhere —
judgment, horrifying visions, and excretions.

Here women are swallowed by this up to their necks,   35.20
and are punished with great pain. These are they
who procured abortions and ruined the work God created.

Opposite them is another place where the children sit,   35.21
but they are alive, and they cry to God.
And lightnings go forth from those children,
which pierce the eyes of those who, by fornication,
brought about their destruction.

Other men and women stand above them naked,   35.22
as their children stand opposite them in a place of delight.
And they sigh and cry to God because of their parents,
"These are they who neglected and cursed and transgressed
your commandment. They killed us and cursed the angel
who created us and hung us up. They withheld from us
the light which you have appointed for all."

And the milk of the mothers flows from their breasts,   35.23
and congeals and smells foul. And from it come forth
beasts that devour flesh, that turn and torture them
and their husbands forever because they forsook the
commandment of God and killed their children.

And the children shall be given to the angel Temlakos.
And those who slew them will be tortured forever,
for God wills it to be so.

35.24

Ezrael, the angel of wrath, brings men and women
with half of their bodies burning
and casts them into a place of darkness — the Hell of men.

35.25

And a spirit of wrath chastises them with all manner
of chastisement, and a worm that never sleeps
consumes their entrails. These are the persecutors
and betrayers of my righteous ones.

35.26

And near to those who live thus are other men and women
who chew their tongues, and they are tormented
with red hot irons and have their eyes burned. These are
the slanderers and those who doubt my righteousness.

35.27

Other men and women — whose deeds were done
in deception — have their lips cut off,
and fire enters their mouths and entrails.
These are those who slew the martyrs by their lying.

35.28

In a place near them is a stone pillar of fire, and the pillar
is sharper than swords, and men and women clad in rags
and filthy garments are cast upon it to suffer the judgment
of unceasing torture. These are they who trusted in their
riches, and despised widows and orphans in the sight of God.

35.29

And into another place near by, saturated with filth,
they throw men and women up to their knees.
These are they who lent money and took usury.

35.30

Other men and women throw themselves down from a high
place and return again and run, and demons drive them.
These are the worshipers of idols, and they drive them to the
end of their wits and they plunge further down from there.
This they do continually, and are tormented forever.

35.31

These are they who have cut their flesh as apostles of a man,   35.32
and the women who were with them, and also those men who
defiled themselves with one another in the fashion of women.

And beneath them the angel Ezrael prepares a place   35.33
of much fire, and all the gold and silver idols — all idols,
the works of men's hands, and what resembles the images
of cats and lions, of reptiles and wild beasts, and the men
and women who manufactured the images — shall be in chains
of fire. They shall be chastised because of their error
before these idols, and this is their judgment forever.

And near them other men and women burn in the flame   35.34
of the judgment, whose torture is forever. These are they
who have forsaken the commandment of God
and followed the ways of the devils.

And from another very high place, the men and women   35.35
who make false steps roll down to where the fear is.
And while the fire that is prepared flows, they mount up
and fall down again, and continue their rolling.
They shall be punished thus forever.

These are they who have not honored their father and mother,   35.36
and of their own accord withdrew themselves from them.
Therefore shall they be punished eternally.

Furthermore the angel Ezrael brings children and maidens   35.37
to show to them those who are punished.
They will be punished with pain, with hanging up,
and with many wounds that flesh-eating birds inflict.

These are they who have confidence in their sins,   35.38
who are not obedient to their parents, who do not follow
the instruction of their fathers, and do not honor
those who are older than they.

Beside them, maidens clad in darkness for raiment will be   35.39
punished and their flesh torn in pieces. These are they who
retained not their virginity until they were given in marriage.
They shall be punished with tortures while they feel them.

And again other men and women who ceaselessly   35.40
chew their tongues and are tormented with eternal fire.
These are the slaves who were not obedient to their masters.
This then is their judgment forever.

And near to this torment are blind and dumb men and   35.41
women whose raiment is white. They are packed closely
together and fall on coals of unquenchable fire. These are they
who give alms and say, "We are righteous before God,"
while they yet have not striven for righteousness. The angel
of God, Ezrael, allows them to come forth out of this fire and
sets forth a judgment of decision. This then is their judgment.

And a stream of fire flows, and all those judged are drawn into   35.42
the midst of the stream. And Uriel sets them down there.
And there are wheels of fire, and men and women hung
thereon by the power of their whirling. These wheels are
without number and the decision is always fire.
Those in the pit burn. These are the sorcerers and sorceresses.

And the angels will bring my elect, who are perfect   35.43
in all righteousness, and shall hold them in their hands
and clothe them with the garment of eternal Life.

They shall see the desires of those who hated them   35.44
as they are punished. Torment for everyone is forever
according to his deeds, and all those who are in torment
will say with one voice, "Have mercy upon us,
for now we know the judgment of God, which he declared
to us beforehand but we did not believe."

And the angel Tatirokos will come and chasten them   35.45
with even greater torment and say unto them,
"Now you repent, when there is no more time for repentance,
and nothing of life remains."

And all shall say, "Righteous is the judgment of God.   35.46
For we have heard and perceived that his judgment is good,
since we are punished according to our deeds."

36. The Seven Churches

I am Alpha and Omega,
the beginning and the end,
the first and the last.

                    36.1

What you see, write in a book
and send it to the seven churches of Asia.
Send it to Ephesus, and Smyrna, and Pergamos,
and Thyatira, and Sardis, and Philadelphia, and Laodicea.

                    36.2

Fear not. I am the first and the last, the Living One.
I am he who was dead, and behold, I am alive forevermore.
I hold the keys of Hell and of death.

                    36.3

Write the things you see, and the things that are,
and the things that shall be hereafter.

                    36.4

The secret meaning of the seven stars you see
in my right hand, and the seven golden lampstands, is this:
The seven stars are the angels of the seven churches.
The seven golden lampstands are the seven churches.

                    36.5

To the angel of the church in Ephesus write,
these are the words of him who holds the seven stars
in his right hand, of him who walks among
the seven golden lampstands:

                    36.6

I know your works, your toil, and your patient endurance.
I know you do not tolerate the wicked.
I know you have tested those who call themselves apostles
but are not, and exposed them as liars.
I know you are enduring patiently and bearing up
for my name's sake, and that you have not grown weary.

                    36.7

But I count one thing against you.   36.8
You have forgotten the first love.
Remember how you were and see how far you have fallen.
Repent, and love as you first did.
If not, if your heart yet remains unchanged,
I will come quickly and remove your lampstand.

But I count one thing for you.   36.9
You hate the deeds of the Nicolaitans, which I also hate.

He who has an ear to hear,   36.10
let him hear what the Spirit says to the churches.
He who triumphs shall be invited to eat of the Tree of Life
in the paradise of God.

To the angel of the church in Smyrna write,   36.11
these are the words of the first and the last,
who died and came to life:

I know of your afflictions and poverty — but you are rich! —   36.12
and of the slander you endure from those who say they
are Jews but are not, who are in fact a synagogue of Satan.

Do not fear what you are about to suffer.   36.13
The devil will throw some of your number into prison,
that you may be tried and tested, and for ten days
you will suffer tribulation. But if you are faithful,
even unto death, you will be given the crown of Life.

He who has an ear to hear,   36.14
let him hear what the Spirit says to the churches.
He who triumphs will not be harmed by the second death.

To the angel of the church in Pergamos write,   36.15
these are the words of him who carries the sword
with two sharp edges:

I know you dwell where Satan has his throne, yet you still   36.16
hold fast my name. And you did not deny my faith,
even in the days of Antipas, my faithful martyr,
who was put to death among you, there where Satan dwells.

But I have a few things against you.   36.17
You tolerate those who follow the teaching of Balaam,
who taught Balak to entice the sons of Israel to stumble,
to eat food sacrificed to idols, and to practice immorality.

And you tolerate those who follow the teaching   36.18
of the Nicolaitans, which I hate. Therefore repent.
If not, I will come to you quickly and war against those
you tolerate with the sword of my mouth.

He who has an ear to hear,   36.19
let him hear what the Spirit says to the churches.
He who triumphs will receive hidden manna, and be given
a white stone with a new name engraved upon it,
that no one understands except he who receives it.

To the angel of the church in Thyatira write,   36.20
these are the words of the Son of God,
who has eyes like the flame of fire,
and whose feet shine like polished bronze:

I know your works, your love and your faith,   36.21
your service and patient endurance,
and that your latter works are even greater than your first.

But this I have against you.   36.22
You tolerate the woman called Jezebel, who calls herself
a prophetess, yet seduces my faithful to practice immorality
and eat food sacrificed to idols. I gave her time to repent,
but she refuses to turn away from harlotry.

Truly, I will cast her onto a bed of suffering,   36.23
and those who commit adultery with her will be thrown into
great tribulation unless they repent of her ways.

I will strike her children dead. And all the churches   36.24
will know that I am he who sees the mind and heart,
and who will assign to each of you what your deeds deserve.

To the rest of you in Thyatira, those who do not hold   36.25
to her ways, who have not sought to learn
the so-called deep secrets of Satan, to you I say,
I lay upon you no other burden.
Only hold fast to what you have until I come.

He who triumphs and keeps my Word until the end   36.26
will be given authority over all the nations,
just as I myself receive authority from God the Father.
And he will rule the nations with an iron scepter,
and they shall be broken like pottery to shivers.

He who has an ear to hear,   36.27
let him hear what the Spirit says to the churches.
I will give him the morning star.

To the angel of the church in Sardis write,   36.28
these are the words of him who has the seven spirits of God
and the seven stars:

I know your works. You have a name like one who lives,   36.29
but you are dead. Wake up!
Strengthen what remains, for it is about to face death,
and your work is not complete in the sight of God.

Remember what you have heard and received from me.   36.30
Keep it and repent! If you do not wake up,
I will come at you like a thief, and you will not know
what hour I come against you.

Even so, you still have a few good names in Sardis,   36.31
people who have not soiled their garments.
They will walk with me in white, for they are worthy.

He who triumphs will be clothed thus, in white raiment.   36.32
I will not blot out his name from the Book of Life,
but will confess him before the Father and all his angels.

He who has an ear to hear,   36.33
let him hear what the Spirit says to the churches.
I will speak his name before God and all the angels.

To the angel of the church in Philadelphia write,   36.34
these are the words of the Holy One, the True One,
who has the key of David, who opens and no one shuts,
who shuts and no one opens:

I know your works. I know you have some strength,   36.35
and you have kept my Word and have not denied my name.
Behold, I open a door for you that no one can shut.

Those of the synagogue of Satan, who lie that they are Jews   36.36
but are not, I will make bow down before your feet,
and they will know that I love you.

Because you have kept my Word with patient endurance,   36.37
I will keep you from the hour of trial that is coming upon
the world to test those who dwell on earth.

I am coming soon. Hold fast to what you have so that none   36.38
may seize your crown. He who triumphs shall become a pillar
in the temple of God, and never shall he have to leave it.

I will write on him the name of God,   36.39
and the name of the city of God, the new Jerusalem,
that comes from God in Heaven.

He who has an ear to hear,   36.40
let him hear what the Spirit says to the churches.
I will write on him my own new name.

To the angel of the church in Laodicea write,   36.41
these are the words of the Amen, the faithful and true witness,
the beginning of God's creation:

I know your works. You are neither cold nor hot.   36.42
Would that you were either cold or hot!
So, because you are lukewarm, and neither hot nor cold,
I spit you out of my mouth.

You say, "I am rich. I have prospered, and I need nothing,"   36.43
not realizing you are wretched, pitiable, poor, blind, naked.

I counseled you to receive from me gold refined by fire   36.44
so that you may be rich, and white garments so that you
might clothe yourself and your nakedness not be seen,
and salve to anoint your eyes so that you might see.

Those I love, I reprove and discipline. Be zealous and repent.   36.45
Behold, I stand at your door and knock.
Whoever hears my knock and opens the door,
I will come in and eat with him, and he with me.

And him who overcomes,   36.46
I will grant to sit with me on my throne,
as I also overcame and sit with my Father on his throne.

He who has an ear to hear,   36.47
let him hear what the Spirit says to the churches.
It is done.

I am the root and the offspring of David,   36.48
and the bright morning star. I sent my angel to testify to you
about these things concerning the churches.

Come closer now and I will reveal to you what lies ahead.   36.49
Take up the book that lies open in the hand of the angel
who stands upon the sea and earth.

Write, for these words are true and faithful: 36.50

Blessed are they who keep my Word,   36.51
for they shall pass through the gates into the Kingdom,
and become unto the Tree of Life.

The kingdom of God is with men.   36.52
He dwells with them and they are his people.
Truly, the home of God is within you, for he is your God.
And he himself shall wipe every tear from your eyes.

Death shall be no more. Neither shall there be sorrow,   36.53
nor crying, nor suffering, nor pain,
for the former things shall all pass away.

Behold, I make all things new.   36.54
He who overcomes shall inherit all good things,
and I will be his God, and he will be my Son.

But the fearful and unbelieving, the abominable   36.55
and murderous, the whoremongers and sorcerers,
the idolaters and those who love lies, these shall inherit
their part in the lake that burns with fire and brimstone.
This is the second death.

Watch therefore, for I come suddenly, and my judgment   36.56
comes with me. Truly, every man shall be rewarded
or punished according to his works.

I am Alpha and Omega, the beginning and the end.   36.57
To him who thirsts for righteousness,
I give water from the Fountain of Life.

Chapter VII
Cosmology

The Coming
The Great Wisdom
Cross of Light
Archons and Ennoias
The Pleroma of Truth

The sermons in Part VII are composed of sayings attributed to Jesus in Gnostic texts that contain a detailed cosmology to explain God, Man, Creation, and the coming of the Christ. These works express the essence of Gnostic myth and revelation, and suggest the life of vision and mysticism that vitalized early Christianity—a life later suppressed then largely forgotten. With the rediscovery of these gospels we have been granted valuable insight into a lost yet fundamental foundation of the Christian tradition.

The vocabulary and "cast of characters" in these texts is quite different from that of the canonical gospels, partly because they arose from a different Christian sect, partly because they have not been sanitized by numerous translations and versionings. The fortunate result is that within these gospels are found some of the most mysterious and illuminating passages in any of the source texts.

Two of these sermons, "The Great Wisdom," and "Archons and Ennoias," contain single works in their entirety because the texts consist almost exclusively of words attributed to Jesus. Some of the sayings in these two sermons also appear elsewhere in *Christ Sutras* where they seemed appropriate to a particular teaching.

37. The Coming

I come as the sun bursting forth. Shining seven times brighter   37.1
than the sun in glory, carried on the wings of the clouds
in splendor with my cross before me,
I come to the earth to judge the living and the dead.

While I was coming from the Father of All,   37.2
I passed through the heavens, wherein I took on the wisdom
of the Father, and by his power, clothed myself in his power.

I passed by the angels and archangels as one of them,   37.3
in their form. I passed by the orders, dominions, and princes,
possessing the wisdom of the Father who sent me.

And the archangels Michael and Gabriel, Raphael and Uriel,   37.4
followed me until the fifth firmament of heaven
while I appeared as one of them.
This kind of power was given me by the Father.

Then I made the archangels become distracted with the voice,   37.5
and go up to the altar of the Father, and serve the Father
in his work until I should return to him.

I did this in the likeness of his wisdom.   37.6
I became All in all of them. And I, having the will
and the mercy of the Father, having perfected the glory
of him who sent me, shall return to him.

I became like an angel to the angels. I appeared in the form   37.7
of the archangel Gabriel to the virgin Mary,
and spoke with her, and her heart received me.

She believed and laughed. And I, the Word, went into her   37.8
and became flesh. And I myself was servant for myself,
in the form of the image of an angel.
So I will do after I have gone to the Father.

I have commanded you to follow me,   37.9
and have taught you what to say before the archons.
I have descended and spoken, and undergone tribulation
and carried off my crown after saving you.

For I came down to dwell with you so that you in turn   37.10
might dwell with me. And finding your houses unceiled,
I have made my abode in the dwellings
that could receive me at the time of my descent.

Those who love me, and who find fault with men   37.11
who do not follow my Way, will be hated and persecuted,
and men will despise and mock them.
They will also deliberately say what is not true,
and there will come a conspiracy against those who love me.
But others will rebuke them that they may be saved.

Those who find fault with men, who correct and exhort them,   37.12
will be hated and set apart and despised, and any who wish
to do good to them will be prevented from it.

Those who have endured this will be as martyrs   37.13
with the Father, for they were zealous concerning
righteousness, and were not zealous with corruption.

Adam was given the power that he might choose   37.14
between darkness and Light. He chose the Light,
and stretched out his hand and took it,
and withdrew from the darkness.
Likewise every man is given the power to choose the Light.
This is the Life of our Father who sent me.

I will give to my elect and righteous the baptism   37.15
and salvation for which they have besought me,
in the field Akrosja, which is called Aneslasleja.

They shall adorn with flowers the ranks of the righteous   37.16
and I will rejoice with them. I will cause the righteous to enter
the eternal Kingdom and reveal to them the eternal things
in which I have given them hope, I and our Father in Heaven.

38. The Great Wisdom
The Sophia of Jesus the Christ

Peace be to you. My peace I give you. 38.1
What are you thinking about? Are you perplexed?
What are you searching for?
"For the underlying reality of the universe and the plan."

All men born from the foundation of the world until now 38.2
are dust. While they have inquired about God,
who he is and what he is like, they have not found him.

The wisest among them have speculated about Truth 38.3
from the ordering of the world and its movements.
But speculation has not reached Truth.
For these philosophers hold three different opinions
about the ordering of the world, and hence they do not agree.

Some say the world is directed by itself. 38.4
Others say that providence directs it. Others say it is fate.
But it is none of these.

Of these three voices, none is true, for they are from man. 38.5
But I who come from Infinite Light am here. I know Light,
and I can speak to you about the precise nature of Truth.

Whatever is from itself is an imitation life, being self-made. 38.6
Providence has no wisdom in it. Fate does not discern.

Now as for you, whatever is fitting for those who are worthy 38.7
of this Knowledge, it will be given to you — not to you who was
begotten by intercourse, but to you the First who
was sent, for you are immortal in the midst of mortal men.

"Lord, teach us the truth." 38.8
He Who Is, is ineffable. No principle knows him, no authority,
no subjection, nor any creature from the foundation of the
world until now, except he alone, and anyone to whom he wills
to reveal himself through him who is from Infinite Light.
Forevermore, I offer this great Salvation.

He Who Is, is immortal and eternal, having never been born.   38.9
Everything that is born will perish.
He is unbegotten, having no beginning.
Everything that has a beginning has an end.

Because no one rules over him he has no name.   38.10
Whatever has a name is the creation of another.
He is unperceivable. He has no form.
Whatever has form is the creation of another.

He has a semblance of his own —   38.11
not like any you have perceived or thought —
but a strange semblance that surpasses all things
and is greater than the universe.
It looks to every side and sees itself from itself.

He is infinite and ever incomprehensible.   38.12
He is unchanging good.
He is faultless. He is timeless.
He is imperishable and has no likeness to anything.
He is eternally blessed.

He is not knowable, yet he ever knows himself.   38.13
He is immeasurable. He is untraceable.
He is perfect, having no defect.
He is called, "Father of the Universe."

"Lord, how, then, does he appear to the perfect ones?"   38.14
Before anything that now appears becomes visible,
the majesty and the authority are in the Father.
He encompasses the whole of Totality.
Nothing encompasses him.

He is all mind, and all thought, and all reflecting,   38.15
and all authority, and all will. These are equal powers.
They are the sources of Totality.

And the whole of Creation, from first to last, is in his   38.16
foreknowledge, that of the infinite Unbegotten Father.

"Lord, how does all this come to be, and why is it revealed?"   38.17
I come from the boundless One
so that I might tell you all things. The One Who Is, is a begetter.
He has the power to beget and create forms,
so that the great wealth contained in him might be revealed.

Because of his mercy and his love, he wishes to bring forth fruit   38.18
of himself so that he might not be alone in the enjoyment
of his goodness, but that other spirits of the unwavering realm
might bring forth body and fruit, glory and honor,
in his imperishableness and unending grace.

In this way is his treasure revealed by Unbegotten God,   38.19
Father of every imperishableness, and of all that henceforth
shall come to be but has not yet appeared.

Whoever has ears to hear about infinities, let him hear!   38.20
It is those who are awake that I address.
I come from the One that I might tell you all things.

A great difference exists between the imperishables   38.21
and those who will perish. Everything that comes from
the perishable will perish, since it comes from the perishable.
But whatever comes from imperishableness does not perish,
but itself becomes imperishable.

The multitude of men go astray   38.22
because they do not know this difference. And they die.

"Lord, how will we come to know that?"   38.23
Beginning with invisibleness you arrive at that which is visible.
The very source of Thought will reveal to you
how faith in the invisible is found in that which is visible,
that which emanates from the Unbegotten Father.

The Lord of the Universe is called not only Father,   38.24
but Forefather, the Source of all appearances,
the beginning-less First Father.
Seeing himself within himself as in a mirror,
he appears, resembling himself.

His likeness is of the divine Self-Father,   38.25
for he is the Confronter of the confronted One,
the first-existing Unbegotten Father.
He is of equal age with the Light before him,
but not equal to it in power.

And then there appears a whole multitude of confronting,   38.26
self-begotten ones, equal in age and power,
being in glory and without number, whose nation is called
"The Generation Over Whom There Is No Kingdom,"
the generation in which you yourself have appeared.

And this whole multitude over which there is no kingdom   38.27
is called "Sons of the Unbegotten Father," or "Sons of God,"
for his likeness is you. Yet he is unknowable,
he who is full of timeless, imperishable glory and ineffable joy.

All are at rest in him, ever rejoicing in ineffable joy, and such   38.28
unchanging glory and measureless jubilation as has never been
heard or known among all the aeons and their worlds.

"Lord, how was man revealed?"   38.29
He who appears before the Universe in Infinity,
the Self-Grown, Self-Constructed Father,
being ineffable and full of shining Light,
decided to have his likeness become a great power.

Immediately, that Light created the appearance of   38.30
androgynous Immortal Man, that through Immortal Man—
through this Interpreter who is with you until the end
of the poverty of the robbers—men might attain their salvation
and awake from forgetfulness.

His consort is the Great Sophia, who the Unbegotten Father   38.31
destined for union in Immortal Man from the first,
and who also appeared as First, and Divinity, and Kingdom.

The Father, who appears as "Man, Self-Father," revealed this.   38.32
And for his own majesty he created a great aeon,
whose name is Ogdoad, who was given great authority
to rule over this Creation of poverty.

184

And from that Light and the tri-male Spirit, that of Sophia,   38.33
his consort, he created gods and angels and archangels,
myriads without number for his retinue.
And from these, God originated Divinity and Kingdom.
Thus he is called "God of Gods," and "King of Kings."

First Man has his unique mind within, and thought—   38.34
for he *is* thought—and considering, and reflecting,
and rationality, and authority.
All of his attributes are perfect and immortal.

In respect to imperishableness, God and Immortal Man   38.35
are equal. But in respect to power, they are different,
like the difference between father and son, or between
son and thought, or between thought and no-thought.
Among all things, God, the One, is primary.

All that exists is created from his power.   38.36
From what is created appears what is fashioned.
From what is fashioned appears what is formed.
From what is formed appears what is named.
Thus arises the separation of the begotten ones,
from beginning to end.

"How is it that he is called "Man," and "Son of Man"?   38.37
To which is this Son related?"
First Man is called Begetter, Self-Perfected Mind.
He reflected with the great Sophia, his consort,
and created First-Begotten, an androgynous son.

His male name is First Begetter, Son of God.   38.38
His female name is First Begettress Sophia,
Mother of the Universe. Some call her Love.

Now First Begotten is called Christ.   38.39
Since he has authority from the Father,
he created a multitude of angels for his retinue,
myriad without number, from Spirit and Light.

"Lord, tell us about the one called Man, that we may know   38.40
  his glory exactly."
First Begetter Father is called Adam, Eye of Light.
He came from shining Light, and his holy angels,
who are ineffable and shadowless, ever rejoice with joy
in their reflecting, which they received from the Father.

The whole kingdom of Son of Man, who is also Son of God,   38.41
is full of ineffable, shadowless joy and unchanging jubilation.
All rejoice in an imperishable glory that is heard only now.
Never before was it revealed, nor shall it be revealed
to aeons and worlds to come.

I come from Self-Begotten and First Infinite Light,   38.42
that I might reveal everything to you now.
Whoever has ears to hear, let him hear.

"Lord, tell us clearly how they came down from the invisibilities,   38.43
from the immortal to the world that dies?"
Son of Man reflected with Sophia, his consort,
and revealed a great androgynous light.
His male name is Savior, Begetter of All Things.
His female name is All-Begettress Sophia. Some call her Faith.

All who come into the world, like a drop from the Light,   38.44
are born into the Creation of the Almighty,
that they might be guarded by him.

And the will of Sophia binds them to forgetfulness   38.45
so that the whole Creation of poverty might be revealed.
For it is the Almighty's arrogance, blindness, and ignorance
that takes a name.

But I come from on high by the will of the great Light.   38.46
I escaped from bondage and cut off the bond of the robbers.
I awakened that drop which was sent from Sophia,
that it might bear much fruit through me,
and be perfected, and not again become defective,
but be united in me, the great Savior.

In this way his glory might be revealed.   38.47
And Sophia might also be corrected of that defect,
that her sons might not again become defective,
but might attain honor and glory, and go to the Father,
and know the words of the masculine Light.

You are sent by the Son.   38.48
The Son is sent that you might receive Light,
and remove yourselves from the ignorance of the authorities.
And so that this Creation of poverty
might not again come into appearance because of you,
because of the intercourse that proceeds from the fire
of the flesh. Tread upon their malicious intent.

"Lord, how many are the aeons of those who surpass the heavens?"   38.49
I praise you because you ask about the great aeons,
for your roots are in the infinities.
After those whom I discussed earlier were revealed,
Self-Begetter Father created twelve aeons for retinue
for the twelve angels. All these are perfect and good.
Thus the defect of the female appeared.

"How many are the aeons of the immortals,   38.50
starting from the infinities?"
The first aeon is that of Son of Man, who is called
First Begetter, who is also called Savior. The second aeon
is that of Man, who is called Adam, Eye of Light.
That which embraces these is the aeon over which
there is no kingdom, the aeon of the Eternal Infinite God,
the Self-Begotten aeon of the aeons,
the aeon of the immortals, the aeon above the Eighth
that appears from Sophia, which is the first aeon.

Immortal Man revealed aeons and powers and kingdoms,   38.51
and gave authority to all who appear in him,
that they might exercise their desires until the last things,
until the days that are above chaos.

These consent with each other and reveal every magnificence,   38.52
even from spirit — multitudinous lights that are glorious
and without number. These were named from the beginning,
that is, the first aeon and the second and the third.

Each one has its own name. The first is called Unity,   38.53
the second Rest. The third aeon is called Assembly,
because of the great multitude that is revealed.
In One, the multitudes appear.

Because the multitudes gather and come to Unity we call them   38.54
Assembly of the Eighth. It appears as androgynous
and is named partly as male and partly as female.

The male is called Assembly. The female is called Life,   38.55
to show that from the female came life for all the aeons.
From the beginning each received a name.
And from his concurrence with Thought,
powers soon appeared who were called "gods."

The gods of the gods, from their authority revealed gods.   38.56
The gods from their wisdom revealed lords.
The lords of the lords from their thoughts revealed lords.
The lords from their power revealed archangels,
and the archangels from their words revealed angels.

From them, semblances appeared, with structure and forms   38.57
and names for all the aeons and their worlds.
And these immortals have authority from Immortal Man,
who as Sophia is called Silence, because by reflecting
without speech, her own majesty is perfected.

Since the imperishables had authority, each created   38.58
a great kingdom in the Eighth, and also thrones and temples
and firmaments for their own majesties.
All these come by the will of the Mother of the Universe.

"Lord, tell us about those who are in the aeons,   38.59
since it is necessary for us to seek them."
If you ask about anything, I will tell you.
They created hosts of angels, myriads without number,
for their following and their glory. They created virgin spirits,
the ineffable and unchangeable lights. They have no sickness
nor weakness, only Will. And they came to be in an instant.

Thus in the glory of Immortal Man and Sophia, his consort,   38.60
the aeons were created quickly in the realm of the heavens
and the firmaments, the realm from which the world
and every aeon, and all those that henceforth shall come,
take their pattern for the creation of their likenesses
in the heavens and the chaos of their worlds.

And all natures, starting from the revelation of chaos,   38.61
are now in the Light without shadow, which shines
with indescribable joy and unutterable jubilation.

And they are eternally delighted because of their unchanging   38.62
glory and immeasurable rest. This cannot be said of aeons
that might henceforth come to be, nor of all their powers.

All that I have just said to you, I say that you might   38.63
shine in Light more than these.

"Lord, where did your disciples come from, and where   38.64
are they going, and what should they do here?"
Sophia, Mother of the Universe, the female consort,
desired to bring these to existence by herself,
without her male consort.

But by the will of the Father of the Universe,   38.65
that his unimaginable goodness might be revealed,
he created a curtain between the immortals and those
that come after them, so that in every aeon and chaos
the defect of the female might appear,
and that error would contend with her.

This is the curtain of Spirit. From the aeons above the   38.66
emanations of Light, a drop from Light and Spirit came down
to the lower regions of Almighty in chaos, that their molded
forms might appear from that drop, for it is a reflection of him,
Arch-Begetter, who is called Yaltabaoth.

That drop manifests their molded forms, through the breath,   38.67
as a living soul. It was withered, and it slumbered
in the ignorance of the soul. When it became hot from the
breath of the Great Light of the Male and took thought,
names were received by all who are in the world of chaos,
and all the things in it, through that Immortal One,
when the breath blew into him.

This came about by the will of Mother Sophia   38.68
so that Immortal Man might piece together the garments
for a judgment on the thieves.
And he welcomed the blowing of that breath.

But since he is like a soul, he is not able to take that power   38.69
for himself until the reign of chaos is complete, that is,
until the time determined by the great angel is reached.

I have taught you about Immortal Man and have loosed   38.70
the bonds of the thieves from him. I have broken the gates
of the pitiless ones in their presence. I have humiliated
their malicious intent. And they all have been shamed,
and have risen from their ignorance.

It is for this reason I come here. That you might be joined   38.71
with that Spirit and Breath, and might from two become One,
just as from the first. And that you might yield much fruit
and go to Him Who Is the Source, in ineffable joy and glory
and honor, and grace of the Father of the Universe.

Whoever knows the Father in pure knowledge   38.72
will go to the Father and repose in the Father.
But whoever knows him defectively
will depart to the defect and the rest of the Eighth.

Whoever knows Immortal Spirit of Light in silence, 38.73
through reflecting and consent in Truth,
let him bring me signs of the Invisible One,
and he will become a light in the Spirit of Silence.

Whoever knows Son of Man in knowledge and love, 38.74
let him bring me a sign of Son of Man,
that he might depart to dwell with those in the Eighth.

I have revealed to you the name of the Perfect One, 38.75
the whole will of the Mother of the Holy Angels,
so that the masculine multitude may be completed here.

And so that the infinities might appear in the aeons 38.76
and in those who come to be in the unfathomable wealth
of the Great Invisible Spirit, so that they all might take from
his goodness the wealth of the Rest that has no kingdom.

I come from First Who Was Sent that I might reveal to you 38.77
Him Who Is the Source. Because of the arrogance
of Arch-Begetter and his angels, they say about themselves that
they are gods. I come to remove their blindness, that I might
tell everyone about God, who contains the Universe.

Tread upon their graves. Humiliate their malicious intent. 38.78
Break their yoke and take up mine. I give you authority
over all things as Sons of Light, that you might
tread upon their power with your feet.

39. Cross of Light

There must be one man to hear these things,   39.1
for I need one who is ready to hear.

This Cross of Light is sometimes called Logos.   39.2
Sometimes Mind, sometimes Jesus, sometimes Christ.
Sometimes a door, sometimes a way, sometimes bread.

Sometimes seed, sometimes resurrection, sometimes Son.   39.3
Sometimes Father, sometimes Spirit, sometimes Life.
Sometimes Truth, sometimes Faith, sometimes Grace.
And so it is called for men's sake. But what it truly is,
as known in itself and spoken to us, is this:

It is the distinction of all things, and the strong uplifting   39.4
of what is firmly fixed out of what is unstable,
and the harmony of wisdom, being wisdom in harmony.

But there are places on the right and on the left,   39.5
powers, authorities, principalities, demons, activities,
threatenings, passions, devils, Satan, and the inferior root
from which the nature of transient things proceeds.

This Cross is that which has united all things by the Word,   39.6
and which has separated off that which is transitory
and inferior, and which has compacted all things into One.

But this is not that wooden cross you shall see when you   39.7
go down from here. Nor am I the man who is on that cross,
I whom you do not now see, but only hear my voice.

I was taken to be what I am not, I who am not   39.8
what for others I was. What they will say of me
is mean and unworthy of me.

Since the place of my rest is neither to be seen nor told,   39.9
much more shall I, the Lord of this place,
be neither seen nor told.

The multitude around the cross that is not of one form,   39.10
is the inferior nature, as are those whom you saw in the Cross
if they have not yet one form. Not every member of him
who has come down has yet been gathered together.

But when human nature is taken up, and the nation that comes   39.11
to me and obeys my voice, then he who now hears me shall be
united with this nation, and shall no longer be what he now is,
but shall be above them, as I am. For so long as you do not
call yourself mine, I am not what I am.

But if you hear me, you also as hearer shall be as I am,   39.12
and I shall be what I was, when you are as I am with myself.
For from me, you are what I am.

Therefore ignore the many and despise those   39.13
who are outside the mystery. For you must know
that I am wholly with the Father, and the Father with me.

40. Archons and Ennoias
The Second Treatise of the Great Seth

I.
The perfect Majesty is at rest in the ineffable Light,   40.1
in the Truth of the Mother of all these, and of all
who attain to me, the perfect One, because of the Word.

I contain all the greatness of Spirit, which is a friend to us   40.2
and our kindred alike. Through the goodness of our Father
I bring forth the glory of his Word. And I bring forth
an imperishable thought, which is the Word
within the Father. It is slavery that dies in Christ.

I bring forth an imperishable and undefiled thought,   40.3
an incomprehensible marvel, which is written in the ineffable
water of my Word: I am in you, and you are in me,
just as the Father is in you, in innocence.

II.
I said, "Let us gather the Assembly. Let us send someone   40.4
forth to visit that lower Creation of his, just as he visited the
ennoias, the thought-images, in the regions below."

I said these things to the whole multitude   40.5
of the multitudinous Assembly of the rejoicing Majesty.
And the whole house of the Father of Truth
rejoiced that I am the one who is from them.

The ennoias were created by thought that comes from   40.6
the undefiled Spirit and descends upon the water,
the regions below. And they all had a single mind,
since it is out of One. They chose me because I was willing.

Now I come forth to reveal this glory to my kindred   40.7
and my fellow spirits. All those who are in the world
are created by the will of Sophia, who is the consort.
Innocence is not uttered. She asks nothing from the All,
nor from the greatness of the Assembly, nor from the Pleroma.

She was first, and she came forth to prepare monads   40.8
and places for the Son of Light and the fellow workers,
for whom she built bodily dwellings
from the elements of the regions below.

But having been born into an empty glory,   40.9
these bodily dwellings end in destruction,
for they are created by Sophia.
Yet they are prepared to receive the Life-giving Word
of the ineffable Monad, of the great Assembly,
of all who persevere, of all who are in me.

III.
I visited a bodily dwelling.   40.10
I cast out the one who was in it first and I went in.
And the whole multitude of the archons became troubled.
And all the matter of the archons, as well as all the begotten
powers of the earth, were shaken when they saw
the likeness of the Image, for it was harmonized.

I am the one who was in it.   40.11
I do not resemble him who was in it first.
He was an earthly man. I am from beyond the heavens.
I did not refuse them, even to become a Christ, but I did not
manifest myself to them as the love that comes forth from me.
I revealed myself as a stranger to the lower regions.

There was a great disturbance in the whole of earth,   40.12
with confusion and flight, as well as in the plan of the archons —
though some were persuaded when they saw
the wonders accomplished by me.

Yet this whole nation that descended into here fled from me,   40.13
from him who left the throne for the Sophia of Hope,
since she had earlier given the sign concerning me
and all those with me, those of the nation of Adonaios.

Others fled, as if from the Cosmocrator and those with him,   40.14
because they brought every kind of punishment upon me.
And there was doubt in their mind about what they would
counsel concerning me, thinking that Sophia is the whole
greatness, and, moreover, speaking false witness against
the Son of Man and the greatness of the Assembly.

IV.
It is not possible for the archons to know the Father of Truth,   40.15
the Man of Greatness. But they, who received a name
because of a contact with ignorance, which is a burning vessel,
created ignorance to destroy Adam, whom they had formed,
in order to conceal knowledge from those who are like him.

The archons, those of the place of Yaltabaoth,   40.16
manifested the realm of the angels, which humanity seeks,
in order that they may not know the Man of Truth.

Then Adam, whom they had formed, appeared to them.   40.17
And a fearful motion arose throughout their entire realm,
lest the angels surrounding them rebel and not offer praise.
I did not really die, lest their archangel become empty.

And then the voice of the Cosmocrator came to the angels,   40.18
saying, "I am God and there is no other beside me."
And I laughed joyfully when I saw his empty glory.
He went on to say, "Who is man?"
And the entire host of his angels, who had seen Adam
and his bodily dwelling, laughed at his smallness.

Thus did their ennoias come to be removed from   40.19
the Majesty of Heaven, from the Man of Truth.
They took a name and a small dwelling place.
They are small and senseless in their empty ennoias
and their laughter. It is contagion for them.

V.
The whole greatness of the Fatherhood of the Spirit   40.20
is at rest in his places. I am he who is with him.
I have an ennoia of a single emanation from the eternal One,
and the undefiled and immeasurable incomprehensibilities.

196

I placed this small ennoia in the world, which disturbed and   40.21
frightened the whole multitude of the angels and their ruler.
I visited them all with fire and flame because of my ennoia.
Everything concerning them was manifested because of me.

And there came about a disturbance and a fight around the   40.22
Seraphim and Cherubim, whose glory will fade, and confusion
around Adonaios on both sides, and their dwelling.
To the Cosmocrator and him who said, "Let us seize him,"
others said, "That plan will certainly not come about."

Adonaios knows me because of hope. I entered into   40.23
the mouths of lions — and the plan they had devised for me —
in order to release them from error and senselessness.
But I did not succumb to them as they planned.
I was not afflicted at all.

Those who were there punished me.   40.24
But I did not die in reality, only in appearance,
lest I be put to shame before my kindred. I removed
the shame from me and I did not become fainthearted
in the face of what happened to me at their hands.

I was about to succumb to fear, and I did suffer according to   40.25
their sight and thought, in order that they may never find any
word to speak of it. But my death, which they think happened
to me, happened to them in their error and blindness.
They nailed their own manhood unto their own death.

Their ennoias did not see me, for they were deaf and blind.   40.26
In doing these things, they condemned themselves.
Yes, they saw me and they punished me. But it was another,
the Father, who drank the gall and vinegar. It was not me.

They struck me with the reed, but it was another   40.27
who bore the cross upon his shoulder. It was another
upon whom they placed the crown of thorns.

I was rejoicing in the height beyond all the wealth of the   40.28
archons and the offspring of their error, of their empty glory.
And I was laughing at their ignorance.
And I subjected all their powers.

VI.
As I descended into this lower region no one saw me.   40.29
I altered my shapes, changing from form to form.
And when I was at their gates, I assumed their likeness.
I passed them by quietly, and looked at all the places.
And I was not afraid nor ashamed, for I was undefiled.

I spoke with them, and mingled with them   40.30
through those who are mine. I trampled on those
who are harsh to those who are mine. I quenched the flame.
I did all these things because I came to accomplish
what is desired by the will of the Father.

The Son of Majesty, who is concealed in the lower regions,   40.31
is raised to the height where I am in all these aeons,
the height no one has ever seen or known,
the height where the wedding of the wedding robe is —
the new one, not the old, the one that does not perish.
For it is a new and perfect bridal chamber of the heavens.

VII.
I have revealed that there are three conditions: 40.32
an undefiled mystery in a spirit of this aeon does not perish,
nor is it fragmentary, nor is it able to be spoken of.
Rather, it is undivided, universal, and permanent.

For the soul, the one from the height, will not speak   40.33
about the error which is here, nor transmit from these aeons.
It will be transmitted when the soul becomes free,
when it is endowed with nobility in the world
and stands before the Father without weariness or fear,
mixed with the Nous of power and form.
They will see me from all sides without hatred.

Since they saw me, they were seen, and I mingled with them.   40.34
Since they did not put me to shame, they were not put to shame.
Since they were not afraid before me, they will pass by
every gate without fear, and will be perfected in the third glory.

It was my going to the revealed height that the world   40.35
did not accept—my third baptism in a manifest image.
When they fled from the fire of the seven Authorities,
and when the sun of the powers of the archons had set,
darkness took them.

VIII.
And the world became poor when he was restrained   40.36
with a multitude of fetters. They nailed him to the tree,
and they fixed him with four nails of brass.
The veil of his temple he tore with his hands.
It was a trembling that seized the chaos of the earth,
for the souls that were in the sleep below were released.

And they arose. They went about boldly,   40.37
having shed zealous service of ignorance and unlearnedness,
beside the dead tombs, having put on the new man.

They have come to know that perfect blessed One   40.38
of the eternal and incomprehensible Father and infinite Light,
which is I, since I came to my own
and united them with myself.

There is no need for many words. My ennoia   40.39
was with their ennoia, therefore they knew what I know.
We took counsel about the destruction of the archons.
Therefore I did the will of the Father, who is I.

I went forth from my home and came into this world.   40.40
I came into being in the world of bodies.
I was hated and persecuted, not only by those who are ignorant,
but also by those who think they are advancing
the name of Christ. They are unknowing and empty,
not knowing who they are, like dumb animals.

They hate and persecute those who are liberated by me.   40.41
Yet should they shut their mouth, they would weep
with a profitless groaning because they do not fully know me.
Instead, they serve two masters, even a multitude.

But you will become victorious in everything,   40.42
in war and battles, in jealous division and wrath.
In the uprightness of our love we are innocent, pure, and good,
for we are of the mind of the Father, an ineffable mystery.

IX.
It was ludicrous. It is I who bear witness that it was ludicrous.   40.43
The archons do not know that it is an ineffable union
of undefiled Truth, as exists among the sons of Light.
They made an imitation. They proclaimed
a doctrine of lies and a dead man, so as to resemble
the freedom and purity of the perfect Assembly.

They joined themselves with a doctrine of fear and slavery   40.44
and worldly cares. They have abandoned worship.
They are small and ignorant, and do not contain
the nobility of Truth. They hate the one in whom they are,
and love the one in whom they are not.

They do not know the Knowledge of the Greatness,   40.45
that it is from above, from a fountain of Truth,
and that it is not from slavery, jealousy, fear,
and love of worldly matter.

That which is not theirs and that which is theirs,   40.46
they use fearlessly and freely. They do not desire,
because they have authority, and issue law from themselves
over whatever they will.

But those who do not possess him are poor.   40.47
They desire him, yet lead astray those who would become
like those who possess the truth of their freedom.
They buy for us servitude, and fear, and constraint of care.
This is slavery.

He who is constrained by force and threat is protected by God.   40.48
The whole nobility of the Fatherhood is not protected,
only he who is from him without word and constraint.

He is united with his will,   40.49
he who belongs only to the Ennoia of the Fatherhood,
to make it perfect and ineffable through the living water.
He is with you mutually in wisdom,
not only in word of hearing, but in deed and fulfilled word.

The perfect ones are worthy to be established in this way,   40.50
and to be united with me in order that they may not
experience any enmity, but good friendship.
I accomplish everything through the good One, for this is
the union of Truth, that they should have no adversary.

Everyone who brings division is hostile to them all.   40.51
He will learn no wisdom at all because he brings division
and is not a friend. But he who lives in harmony
and friendship of brotherly love, naturally and not artificially,
completely and not partially, is truly living the desire
of the Father. He is the universal One, and perfect Love.

X.
Adam was a laughingstock,   40.52
since he was made a counterfeit type of man by the Hebdomad,
as if he had become stronger than I and my brothers.
We are innocent with respect to him, since we have not sinned.

Abraham, Isaac, and Jacob were a laughingstock, since they,   40.53
the counterfeit fathers, were given a name by the Hebdomad,
as if he had become stronger than I and my brothers.
We are innocent with respect to him, since we have not sinned.

David was a laughingstock in that his son was named   40.54
the Son of Man, having been influenced by the Hebdomad,
as if he had become stronger than I and my brothers.
We are innocent with respect to him. We have not sinned.

Solomon was a laughingstock, since he thought he was Christ,   40.55
having become vain through the Hebdomad,
as if he had become stronger than I and my brothers.
I am innocent with respect to him. I have not sinned.

The twelve prophets were laughingstocks,   40.56
since they have come forth as imitations of the true prophets.
They came into being as counterfeits through the Hebdomad,
as if he had become stronger than I and my brothers.
We are innocent with respect to him. We have not sinned.

Moses, a faithful servant, was a laughingstock,   40.57
having been named "The Friend." They perversely bore
witness concerning him who never knew me. Neither he nor
those before him, from Adam to Moses to John the Baptist,
none of them knew me nor my brothers.

They preach a doctrine of angels imposing dietary laws and   40.58
bitter slavery. They never knew Truth, nor will they know it.
There is a great deception upon their soul, making it impossible
for them to ever find a Nous of freedom to know him,
until they come to know the Son of Man.

Concerning my Father, I am he whom the world did not know.   40.59
Because of this, the world rose up against me and my brothers.
We are innocent with respect to him. We have not sinned.

XI.
The Archon was a laughingstock because he said,   40.60
"I am God, and there is none greater than I. I alone
am the Father, the Lord, and there is no other beside me.
I am a jealous God, who brings the sins of the fathers
upon the children for three and four generations."
As if he had become stronger than I and my brothers!
We are innocent with respect to him. We have not sinned.
We mastered his teaching.

He is in an empty glory. He does not agree with our Father.   40.61
Through our fellowship I grasped his teaching. He is vain
in an empty glory, and he does not agree with our Father.

He is a laughingstock, and judgment, and false prophecy.   40.62
O those who do not see! You do not see your blindness.
You do not see that which is not known,
nor ever was known, nor ever will be known about him.

They did not listen to firm obedience, but proceeded   40.63
in a judgment of error. They raised their defiled and murderous
hands against him, as if they were beating the air.
The senseless and blind ones are always senseless,
always slaves of law and earthly fear.

XII.
I am Christ, the Son of Man,   40.64
the one from you who is among you.
I am despised for your sake in order that you yourselves
might forget the difference. Do not give birth like a female
to evil and its brothers: jealousy, division, anger, wrath, fear,
a divided heart, and empty, non-existent desire.
I am an ineffable mystery to you.

Before the foundation of the world, when the whole multitude   40.65
of the Assembly came together upon the places of the Ogdoad,
they took counsel about a spiritual wedding in Union.

Thus he was perfected in the ineffable places   40.66
by the living Word and the immaculate wedding,
consummated through the Mesotes of Jesus,
who inhabits them all and possesses them,
who abides in undivided love and power.

To those around him he appears as a monad of all these,   40.67
a thought and a father, since he is One.
He is above them all, since he came forth whole and alone.

And he is Life, since he came from the Father   40.68
of ineffable and perfect Truth, the Father of those who are here,
the union of peace and a friend of good things, and life eternal,
and undefiled joy in a great harmony of life and faith,
through eternal life of fatherhood and motherhood
and sisterhood and rational wisdom.

They agreed with Nous, who stretches out and will stretch out   40.69
in joyful union, and is trustworthy, and faithfully listens.
And he is in fatherhood and motherhood and rational
brotherhood and wisdom. This is a wedding of Truth,
a repose of incorruption in a spirit of Truth in every mind,
and a perfect light in an unnamable mystery.

This does not happen among us in any region or place where   40.70
there is division and breach of peace, nor will it. It happens
in union and love, which are perfected in the One Who Is.

It also happens in places under heaven for their reconciliation.   40.71
Those who know me in salvation and undividedness,
who exist for the glory of the Father and the Truth,
having been separated, become One through the living Word.

XIII.
I am in the Spirit and the Truth of the Motherhood,   40.72
just as he is there. I am among those who are united
in the friendship of friends forever, who know neither
hostility nor evil, but who are united by my Word and Peace,
which exists in perfection with everyone, and is in them all.

And those who assume the form of my type will assume   40.73
the form of my Word. Indeed, these will come forth
in light forever, and in friendship with each other in Spirit.
They shall know in every respect with certainty
that what is, is One. And all of these are One.

Thus they shall know the One,   40.74
as did the Assembly and those dwelling in it.
The Father of All exists, immeasurable and immutable:
Nous and Word and Division and Envy and Fire.

He is entirely One, being the All. He is with them all   40.75
in a single principle, because all are from a single Spirit.
O unseeing ones, why do you not know the mystery rightly?

XIV.
The archons around Yaltabaoth were disobedient because of   40.76
the ennoia who went down to him from sister Sophia.
They joined in union with those who were with them
in a fiery cloud of their envy.
The rest were brought forth by their creatures,
as if they had bruised the noble pleasure of the Assembly.

They manifested ignorance in a counterfeit of fire and earth,   40.77
and a murderer. They are small and untaught.
Without knowledge they dared these things, not understanding
that light has fellowship with light, and darkness with darkness,
and the corruptible with the perishable,
and the imperishable with the incorruptible.

XV.
I am Jesus Christ, the Son of Man, who is exalted   40.78
above the heavens. These things I have presented to you,
O perfect and incorruptible ones, because of the incorruptible
and perfect mystery, and the ineffable One.

We decreed them before the foundation of the world,   40.79
so that when we emerge from the places of the world,
we may present the symbols of incorruption
of spiritual union unto Knowledge.

You do not know it because the cloud of flesh   40.80
overshadows you. I alone am the friend of Sophia.
I have been in the bosom of the Father from the beginning,
in the place of the sons of Truth, and the Greatness.
Rest then with me, my fellow spirits and my brothers, forever.

41. The Pleroma of Truth

If the things that are visible in the world are obscure to you, 41.1
how can you hear about the things that are not visible?

If the deeds of truth that are visible in the world 41.2
are difficult for you to perform, how shall you perform
those deeds that pertain to the exalted height
and the pleroma of Truth, which are not visible?

How can you be called "craftsmen"? 41.3
In this respect you are apprentices,
and have not yet received the height of perfection.

All bodies of men and beasts are begotten ignorant. 41.4
Surely this is evident in the way a creature behaves.
However, those that are above are not visible among things
that are visible, but are visible only in their own root.
And it is their fruit that nourishes them.

Visible bodies eat creatures similar to them, 41.5
with the result that the bodies change.
That which changes will decay and perish,
and has no hope of life from then on, since that body is bestial.

Just as the bodies of beasts perish, 41.6
so also will these forms perish. Do they not derive
from intercourse like the bodies of the beasts?
If these bodies, too, derive from intercourse,
how will they beget anything different from beasts?
You are babes until you become perfect.

Truly, as for such as these, do not esteem them as men, 41.7
but regard them as beasts, for just as beasts devour
one another, so also men of this sort devour one another.

They are deprived of the Kingdom because they love 41.8
the sweetness of the fire and are servants of death.
They rush to the works of corruption.
They fulfill the lust of their fathers.

They will be thrown down to the abyss and be afflicted   41.9
by the torment of the bitterness of their evil nature.
They will be scourged so as to make them rush headlong
to the place that they do not know, and they will not recede
from their limbs patiently, but with despair.

They rejoice over the concern for this life with madness   41.10
and derangement. Some pursue this derangement
without realizing their madness, thinking they are wise.

They are beguiled by the beauty of their body,   41.11
as if it would not perish, and they are frenetic.
Their thought is occupied with their deeds,
and thought is the fire that burns them.

For a time determined in proportion to their ignorance,   41.12
they will rule over the little ones. And after the completion
of the error, the never-aging One of immortal understanding
shall become young, and the little ones shall rule
over those who are their rulers.

The root of their ignorance he shall pluck out,   41.13
and he shall put it to shame so that it shall be manifest
in all the impudence which it has assumed to itself.
And such ones shall become unchangeable.

Others who suffer seek to perfect the wisdom of the   41.14
true brotherhood, which is spiritual fellowship with those
united in communion, through which the wedding of
incorruptibility is revealed.

The kindred tribe of the sisterhood appears as an imitation.   41.15
These are the ones who oppress their brothers, saying to them,
"Through this oppression God shows you his pity,
since salvation comes to you through this."

They know not the punishment awaiting those made glad   41.16
by the suffering and imprisonment of innocents.

All that which exists not, dissolves into what exists not.   41.17
The deaf and blind join only with their own kind, but others
shall be saved from evil words and misleading mysteries.

Some who do not understand Mystery speak of things   41.18
they do not understand. They boast that the mystery of Truth
is theirs alone. In haughtiness they grasp in pride
to be envied as an immortal soul that has become a pledge.

For every authority, rule, and power of the aeons   41.19
desires to be with the immortal souls in Creation, in the world,
in order that those who are not, having been forgotten
by those who are, may praise them—though they have not been
saved nor brought to the Way by them—
always wishing that they may become imperishable ones.

Blessed are those above belonging to the Father,   41.20
who revealed Life to those who are from Life,
through me, since I reminded them.

Blessed are they who are built on what is strong, that they   41.21
may hear my Word and distinguish words of righteousness
from words of unrighteousness and transgression of law—
that Word being from the height of every word
of this pleroma of Truth, having been enlightened
in good pleasure by him whom the principalities sought.

But they did not find him, nor was he mentioned among   41.22
any generation of the prophets. Now he has appeared
in the body of him who you see, the Son of Man, who is exalted
above the heavens in a fear of men of like essence.

But you yourself, Peter, become perfect in accordance   41.23
with your name with me, the one who chose you.
Because with you I shall establish a base for others I summon
to Knowledge. Therefore be strong until
the imitation of righteousness of him who summoned you,
who summoned you to know him in a way worth knowing.

Because of the rejection he suffered, and the sinews   41.24
of his hands and his feet, and the crowning by those
of the middle region, and the body of his radiance,
which they bring in hope of service and a reward of honor,
he was about to reprove you three times in this night.

Listen to what I tell you and believe in Truth.   41.25
That which sows and that which is sown
will dissolve in their fire — within the fire and water —
and they will hide in tombs of darkness.

After a long time they shall appear as the fruit of evil trees,   41.26
being punished, being slain in the mouth of beasts and men,
at the instigation of the rains and winds and air,
and the light that shines above.

Evil cannot produce good fruit. For the place in which   41.27
each of them is, produces that which is like itself.
Not every soul is of Truth, nor of immortality.

Every soul of these ages has death assigned to it. It is always   41.28
a slave, created for its desires and eternal destruction —
in which they are, and from which they are.
They love the creatures of matter that come forth with them.

But the immortal souls are not like these.   41.29
Indeed, as long as the hour is not yet come, the immortal soul
resembles a mortal one. It does not reveal its nature —
that it alone is the immortal One and knows immortality —
having Faith, and desiring to renounce these things.

This visible Light shines on your behalf, not in order   41.30
that you remain here, but rather that you come forth.
And whenever all the elect abandon bestiality,
this visible Light will withdraw up to its Essence,
and its Essence will welcome it, since it is a good servant.

Pray that you not come to be in the flesh, but rather that you   41.31
come forth from the bondage of the bitterness of this life.
And as you pray, you will find rest,
for you have left behind the suffering and the disgrace.

When you come forth from the sufferings and passions   41.32
of the body, you will receive rest from the good One,
and you will reign with the King—you joined with him
and he with you—from now on, forever and ever.

These things you understand you shall present to those   41.33
of another nation who are not of this age.
There is no honor in any man who is not immortal,
but only in those who are chosen from an immortal substance,
that is, Him who gives his abundance.

Therefore be courageous and do not fear at all.   41.34
I am with you, and no enemy shall ever prevail over you.
Peace be with you. Be strong!

Chapter VIII

Christhood

Book of Yeshua

What first drew me to begin work on *Christ Sutras* was the possibility of assembling a sermon that summarized the highest teachings of Jesus in his own words, teachings that point directly to the realization of Truth. As I related in the "Introduction," this idea gave way to composing multiple sermons using *all* of his sayings, then returned once that had been completed, eventually manifesting as this final sermon. All the verses used in "Book of Yeshua" are duplicated from other *Christ Sutras* sermons.

Who am I to be choosing which sayings express the highest teachings of Christ? It's a fair question. I have no formal theological training and haven't even been to church much. When I was a kid my mother often expressed how churchgoing was a good thing, but we didn't actually attend very often. For this I give credit to my father. "I feel closer to God outdoors than I do in a pew," he'd say when pressed—a sentiment my child-self instinctively shared and which still resonates true. Once in awhile, though, my mother would take it upon herself to get us to church without him, giving me enough of a taste to know I didn't much care for it, though I do remember feeling a certain curiosity about Jesus himself.

In my teens I embraced a sort of beat-generation nihilism, and by the time I joined the Army I considered religious beliefs to be a sign of ignorance and weakness. But as the cliché goes, there are no atheists in foxholes, and sure enough, whenever things got tense in Vietnam I heard myself praying to God and Jesus and anything else I could remember from the religion of my childhood to *please save my sorry ass!* Mostly this prayer was answered as asked, except once, when it was answered with an explosion that propelled me into a clear and brilliant blackness that felt like *Home*.

In the years that followed I became a "seeker of enlightenment," determined to look in every corner and turn over every rock in search of Truth. Mostly I was drawn to the masters of the east—Buddha, Lao Tsu, Ramana Maharshi, Nisargadatta—but to my surprise Jesus was always there too, in the background, tugging at my heart.

And so it was that somewhere along the way I found myself showing up at Saint Michael's Episcopal on occasional Sunday mornings. What I discovered was that I still did not care much for church. And yet, beneath all the pomp and poppycock there was, I don't know, something. When they stopped making me stand up and sit down every two minutes, inside I got very still. More often than not, I wept taking communion.

I added Christian mystics to my reading list—Meister Eckhart, Saint John of the Cross, Bernadette Roberts. I spent weekends at a Trappist monastery chanting psalms with the monks at all hours. I experienced *mysterium tremendum* in the Gothic cathedrals of Europe. I repeated the Jesus Prayer as a mantra every night as I dropped off to sleep: *Lord Jesus Christ, Son of God, have mercy on me, a sinner.* (A pious version of *please save my sorry ass.*)

Eventually, after thirty-seven years of looking for God in as many ways and places as I could think of, something happened that stopped everything: *The one seeking God is God. There is only God.*

For months afterwards I didn't read anything, or even do anything, really. Just being—joyfully *being*—made up my days. When I was finally moved to read again, I reached for the old masters— Buddha, Jesus, Lao Tsu. What I found was that for the first time I understood what they were trying to say. Yet at the same time I saw how the words themselves obscured what was behind them. It's a laughable Catch 22—you have to become what the words are pointing at before you can understand the words. But once you realize That, you have no use for words! Still, with this new perspective and being trained in writing, I thought I might do a better job of translating some of the ancient eastern texts, which caused me to embark on what became *The Perennial Way.* When it was completed, I began work on *Christ Sutras.*

"Book of Yeshua" conveys what to me are the core teachings of Jesus, and of course I hope it speaks to those who read it. But even more, I hope it inspires you to spend time with *all* the sayings of Jesus and feel which resonate with your own deepest understanding.

> *If you know these things for yourself, they are yours.*
> *If you do not know them for yourself, they are not yours.*

42. Book of Yeshua

Peace to you. My peace I give to you.   42.1

It is necessary I speak to you of certain things,   42.2
because this is the teaching for the perfect.
If you desire to become perfect, you must observe these things.
If not, you shall remain ignorant.

It is impossible for a wise man to dwell with a fool.   42.3
For the wise man is perfect in all wisdom,
while the fool cannot even discern between good and bad.
The wise man is nourished by Truth,
like a tree growing by a meandering stream.

The ignorant, although they have wings, are attracted   42.4
to the visible forms, things that are far from Truth.
For that which drives them, the fire,
gives them an illusion of truth.

It shines on them with perishable beauty,   42.5
imprisons them in dark sweetness,
and captivates them with fragrant pleasure.

It blinds them with insatiable lust and burns their souls.   42.6
It becomes for them a stake in the heart
they can never dislodge. And like a bit in the mouth,
it leads them according to its own desire.

It fetters them with its chains and binds all their limbs   42.7
with the bitter bond of lust for visible things,
things that decay, and change, and swerve by impulse.

They rejoice over the concern for this life with madness   42.8
and derangement. Some pursue this derangement
without realizing their madness, thinking they are wise.

They are beguiled by the beauty of their body, 42.9
as if it would not perish, and they are frenetic.
Their thought is occupied with their deeds,
and thought is the fire that burns them.

The ignorant are always attracted downwards. 42.10
And as they are killed they are assimilated
into the substance of all beasts,
the substance of the perishable realm.

A great difference exists between the imperishable 42.11
and those who will perish.
Everything that comes from the perishable will perish,
for it comes from the perishable.
But whatever comes from the imperishable does not perish,
but itself becomes imperishable.

That flesh comes into being because of spirit is a wonder. 42.12
But if spirit came into being because of the flesh,
it would be a wonder of wonders.
Indeed, I am amazed at how the great wealth of spirit
has made its home in the great poverty of flesh.

Which falls away, flesh or spirit? 42.13
Flesh falls away.

That which you have within you will save you 42.14
if you bring it forth from yourself.
That which you do not have within you will kill you
if you do not have it within you.

All natures, all forms, all creatures exist in and with one 42.15
another, and they are resolved again into their own roots.
For the nature of matter is resolved into
the roots of its nature alone.

He who is from Truth does not die. 42.16
He who is from the womb of woman, dies.
The multitude of men go astray
because they do not know this difference. And they die.

Whoever has ears to hear about infinities, let him hear!   42.17
It is those who are awake that I address.
I come from the One that I might tell you all things.

It is to those who are worthy of my mysteries   42.18
that I tell my mysteries. Whoever finds the truth
of my words will not experience death.

My teaching is not mine, but of the One who sends me.   42.19
He who sees me, sees the One who sends me.
He who receives me, receives the One who sends me.
I come as Light into the world,
that whoever receives me may not remain in darkness.

There is light within a man of Light,   42.20
and he lights up the whole world.
If he does not shine, he is in darkness.
It is in Light that light exists.

I am Alpha and Omega, the beginning and the end.   42.21
Fear not. I am the first and the last, the Living One.
I am he who was dead, and behold, I am alive forevermore.

Before Abraham was, I am.   42.22
All authority is given me, on earth and in Heaven.
I and the Father are One.

I came to make the things below like the things above,   42.23
and the things outside like those inside.
I came to unite them in that Place.

I am the Way, the Truth, and the Life.   42.24
All who come to the Father, come through me.
If you know me, you know the Father.
Henceforth you know him, and have seen him.

It is I who am the Light above the All.   42.25
It is I who am the All.
From me does the All come forth.
Into me does the All extend.

Split a piece of wood and I am there.
Lift up a stone and you will find me.

42.26

He who will drink from my mouth will become like me,
and I myself shall become he,
and the things that are hidden shall be revealed to him.

42.27

I shall give you what no eye has seen,
and what no ear has heard, and what no hand has touched,
and what has never occurred to the human mind.

42.28

I am the Light of the world.
He who becomes as me will not walk in darkness,
but will be the Light of Life.

42.29

He who becomes as me will also do the works that I do,
and greater works than these will he do.

42.30

While you yet have time in the world,
listen to me, and I will reveal to you
the things you have pondered in your mind.

42.31

You have received mercy.
Do you not, then, desire to be filled?
Your heart is drunken.
Do you not, then, desire to be sober?

42.32

If you consider how long the world existed before you,
and how long it will exist after you,
you will find that your life is but one single day,
and your sufferings one single hour.

42.33

If you knew — you, now, in this your day —
the things that make for your peace!
But they are hidden from your eyes.

42.34

While you have the Light, receive the Light,
that you may become sons of Light.

42.35

Take heed of the Living One while you are alive, 42.36
lest you die and seek to know him but be unable to do so.
He who lives from the Living One will not see death.

I know that in faith and with your whole heart 42.37
you question me. Therefore I am glad because of you.
I am truly pleased, and my Father in me rejoices
that you thus inquire and ask. Your boldness makes me
rejoice, and it affords you Life.

Inquire then, and I will tell you all you wish to know, 42.38
and I myself will make known to you what you do not ask.

II.
You ask how your end will be? 42.39
Have you discovered, then, the beginning,
that you look for the end?
Where the beginning is, there also is the end.

Blessed is he who abides in the ever-beginning. 42.40
He will know the end and will not experience death.

Blessed is He Who Is — before everything comes into being. 42.41
For He Who Is, ever has been, and ever shall be.

He Who Is, is ineffable. 42.42
No principle knows him, no authority, no subjection,
nor any creature from the foundation of the world until now,
except he alone, and anyone to whom he wills to reveal
himself through him who is from Infinite Light.
Forevermore, I offer this great Salvation.

He Who Is, is immortal and eternal, having never been born. 42.43
Everything that is born will perish.
He is unbegotten, having no beginning.
Everything that has a beginning has an end.

Because no one rules over him, he has no name. 42.44
Whatever has a name is the creation of another.
He is unperceivable. He has no form.
Whatever has form is the creation of another.

He has a semblance of his own —   42.45
not like any you have perceived or thought —
but a strange semblance that surpasses all things
and is greater than the universe.
It looks to every side and sees itself from itself.

He is infinite and ever incomprehensible.   42.46
He is unchanging good.
He is faultless. He is timeless.
He is imperishable and has no likeness to anything.
He is eternally blessed.

He is not knowable, yet he ever knows himself.   42.47
He is immeasurable. He is untraceable.
He is perfect, having no defect.
He is called, "Father of the Universe."

Before anything that now appears becomes visible,   42.48
the majesty and the authority are in the Father.
He encompasses the whole of Totality.
Nothing encompasses him.

He is all mind, and all thought, and all reflecting,   42.49
and all authority, and all will. These are equal powers.
They are the sources of Totality.

And the whole of Creation, from first to last,   42.50
is in his foreknowledge, that of the infinite, Unbegotten Father.

There comes a time and an hour when what comes next   42.51
is to go to the Father.

What must you do to be doing the work of God, the Father?   42.52
The work of God is to become as him he sends to you.

Take my yoke upon you and learn from me.   42.53
I am gentle and humble in heart,
and you will find rest for your souls.
My yoke is easy and my burden is light.

Come, follow me. I will make you fishers of men.   42.54
Come, follow me. Let the dead bury their dead.

Keep my commandments and follow my Way,   42.55
without reserve, without delay,
without respect of persons.
Walk the straight, direct, and narrow path,
and in every respect the Father will rejoice concerning you.

He who knows and keeps my commandments loves me.   42.56
He who loves me will be loved by my Father,
and I will love him and manifest myself to him.

And if you ask anything in my name, I will do it.   42.57
If you love me, therefore, keep my commandments.

The Lord your God is One.   42.58
You shall love the Lord your God
with all your heart, and with all your soul,
and with all your mind, and with all your strength.
This is the first and greatest commandment.

The second commandment is like it: 42.59
Love your neighbor as yourself.
There are no other commandments greater than these.

As I love you, therefore, love one another.   42.60
By this all men will know you are my disciples,
that you love one another.
Love your brother like your soul.
Guard him like the pupil of your eye.

Do not tell lies. Do not do what you hate.   42.61
For all things are plain in the sight of Heaven.
Nothing hidden will remain unmanifest.
Nothing covered will not be uncovered.

Do not worry about your life, about what you will eat   42.62
or what you will drink, nor about your body,
about what clothing you will put on.
Do not be concerned from morning until evening,
and from evening until morning about what you will wear.

Is not life more than food and the body more than clothing?   42.63
Look at the birds of the air. They neither sow nor reap
nor gather into barns, yet your Father in Heaven feeds them.
Are you not of more value than they?

Therefore, give no thought for tomorrow.   42.64
Let tomorrow come with tomorrow's things.
Sufficient for the day is its own arising.

Love one another and honor each other,   42.65
that continual peace may reign among you.
What you do not want done to you, that do to no one else.

Love your enemies. Do good to those who hate you.   42.66
Bless those who curse you.
Pray for those who spitefully use you.

To him who strikes you on one cheek, turn the other.   42.67
To him who takes your cloak, offer him your tunic.
Give to everyone who asks, and from him who borrows
your goods, do not ask for them back.
As you want men to do to you, do to them likewise.

Be merciful, just as your Father is merciful.   42.68
Judge not, that you not be judged.
Condemn not, that you not be condemned.
Let he who is without sin cast the first stone.
Love your enemies.

For with what judgment you judge, you shall be judged,   42.69
and the measure you give will be the measure you get,
and still more will be given you.

Forgive, and you will be forgiven.
Give, and it will be given to you.
Good measure, pressed down, shaken together
and running over will be put into your bosom.

It is to the good, guileless, sincere ones
that the mystery of death is revealed.
They shall know the Kingdom of those reborn in Christ.

You must become perfect,
just as your Father in Heaven is perfect.

III.
Enter by the narrow gate.
For wide is the gate and broad is the way
that leads to destruction.
And there are many who go in by it.

But strait is the gate and narrow is the way
that leads to Life. And there are few who find it.

Recognize what is in your sight,
and that which is hidden will become plain to you.
For there is nothing hidden that will not become manifest.

Come to hate falsehood and the evil of thought.
For it is thought that gives birth to falsehood,
and falsehood is far from Truth.

Ask and it shall be given you.
Seek and you shall find.
Knock and it shall be opened to you.

For everyone who asks receives, and he who seeks finds,
and to him who knocks, it will be opened.

For the one who speaks is also the one who hears,
and the one who sees is also the one who manifests,
and the one who seeks is also the one who reveals.

42.70
42.71
42.72
42.73
42.74
42.75
42.76
42.77
42.78
42.79

Let him who seeks continue seeking until he finds.   42.80
When he finds, he will become troubled,
and when he becomes troubled he will be astonished,
and he will reign over the All.

Whoever keeps my Word and follows my Way   42.81
will be a son of the Light, a son of God the Father.
It is for the sake of those who keep and do my Word
that I have come from Heaven.

Become earnest about the Word!   42.82
For as to the Word, the first part is Faith,
the second is Love, the third is Works.
From these come Life.

Whoever would become as me, let him deny himself.   42.83
Let him take up his cross and follow me.
For whoever would save his life will lose it,
but whoever loses his life for righteousness sake, will save it.
What shall it profit a man if he gain the whole world,
yet lose his own soul?

Whoever does not forsake all that he has,   42.84
is not a disciple of my Way.
Truly, he who loves his life shall lose it.
But he who renounces his life in this world
shall know eternal Life.

When you leave behind the things that cannot follow you,   42.85
then you will know peace. He who truly wants to enter
the kingdom of Heaven, will enter it.

There is no one who has left house or brother or sister   42.86
or mother or father or children or land for my sake
and for the sake of Truth,
who will not receive a hundredfold, now in this time,
houses and brothers and sisters and mothers and fathers
and children and lands, and in the age to come, eternal Life.
For many who are last will be first, and the first last.

Seek ye first the kingdom of God and his righteousness,   42.87
and all these things shall be added unto you.

The kingdom of God is not found by looking out.   42.88
No one can tell you, "Look here," or "Look there."
The kingdom of God is within you.

The Kingdom will not come by waiting for it. It will not be   42.89
a matter of saying, "I found it," or "There it is."
The kingdom of God is everywhere but you do not see it!

If those who lead you say, "The kingdom of God is in the sky,"   42.90
then the birds of the sky will precede you. If they say to you,
"It is in the sea," then the fish will precede you.
Rather, the kingdom of God is inside you, and before you.

The kingdom of God is with men.   42.91
He dwells with them and they are his people.
Truly, the home of God is within you, for he is your God.
And he himself shall wipe every tear from your eyes.

Death shall be no more. Neither shall there be sorrow,   42.92
nor crying, nor suffering, nor pain,
for the former things shall all pass away.

Have faith and be of good courage.   42.93
Truly I say to you, such a rest will be yours,
where there is no eating, nor drinking, nor mourning,
nor singing, nor care, nor earthly garment, nor death.

You will no longer have your part in the lesser creation,   42.94
but will belong to the incorruptibility of the Father,
and you will not perish.

For you are in Christ always,   42.95
and Christ is always in the Father.

Until now, you have asked nothing in the name of Christ.   42.96
Ask and you will receive, that your joy may be full.
Whatever you ask in prayer, believing, you will receive.

If you can, believe! Do not fear, only believe.   42.97
All things are possible for him who believes.

Truly, if you have but faith the size of a mustard seed,   42.98
you can say to this mulberry tree, "Be pulled up by the roots
and be planted in the sea," and it would obey you.

If you have but faith as a mustard seed,   42.99
you can say to this mountain, "Move from here to there,"
and it will move. Nothing will be impossible for you.

Believe me, whoever says to this mountain, "Be taken up and   42.100
cast into the sea," and does not doubt in his heart, but believes
that what he says will come to pass, it will be done for him.

I tell you, whatever you ask in prayer,   42.101
believe that you have received it, and it will be yours.

The things that are impossible with men   42.102
are possible with God. Have faith in God.

The kingdom of God is when the two become one,   42.103
when that which is without is as that which is within,
when the male and the female are neither male nor female.

For when you make the two, one, you become a son of God.   42.104
And when you say, "Mountain, move away,"
it will move away.

To enter the Kingdom, become like an infant.   42.105
For when you make the two, one,
and make the inside like the outside,
and make the outside like the inside,
and make the above like the below,
and when you make the male and the female
one and the same, so that the male not be male,
nor the female be female,
and when you fashion an eye in place of an eye,
and a hand in place of a hand, and a foot in place of a foot,
and a likeness in place of a likeness,
then will you enter the kingdom of God.

Truly, whoever does not receive the kingdom of God   42.106
as an infant child, shall not enter it.

For the light of the body is the eye.   42.107
If, therefore, your eye is single, your whole body is light.

But if your eye is divided, being part darkness,   42.108
your whole body is darkness.
Take heed, therefore, that the light within you is not darkness.
For if the light that you are is darkness,
how great is that darkness!

He who is undivided is filled with light.   42.109
He who is divided is filled with darkness.

When you come to know yourself,   42.110
you will become what is known, and you will realize
that you are the son of the living Father.

But if you do not know yourself, you dwell in poverty,   42.111
and it is you who are that poverty.
For whoever believes he is less than the All,
is completely ignorant.

He who does not know himself knows nothing.   42.112
But he who knows himself,
at the same time knows the Totality of the All.

Heaven and earth will roll up in your presence.   42.113
For whoever finds himself, contains the world.

It is in this way that you enter the kingdom of Heaven.   42.114
But unless you receive it yourself, through direct knowing,
you will not be able to find it.

Blessed are your eyes, for they see, and your ears,   42.115
for they hear. Truly I say to you, many prophets
and righteous men have desired to see what you see,
yet did not see it, to hear what you hear, yet did not hear it.

No one will ever enter the kingdom of Heaven at my bidding,   42.116
but only because you yourself are whole.
Hearken to the Word, understand Knowledge, love Life.
No one persecutes or oppresses you other than you yourself!

Hasten to be saved without being urged!   42.117
Be eager of your own accord and, if possible,
arrive even before me. Our Father will love you.

Truly, he who receives Life and enters the Kingdom   42.118
will never leave it. Not even the Father can banish him.

Everything I have said to you,   42.119
you have heard and received in faith.
If you know these things for yourself, they are yours.
If you do not know them for yourself, they are not yours.

Be courageous and do not fear at all.   42.120
I am with you, and no enemy shall ever prevail over you.
Peace be with you. Be strong.

See rightly! The kingdom of Heaven is within you!   42.121

Pages from The Gospel of Thomas discovered at Nag Hammadi in 1945

Appendix A: List of Sources

The following abbreviations for the gospels contributing to *Christ Sutras* are used in the cross-reference table in Appendix B.

Abbreviation	**Source Text**
ActsJohn	*Acts of John*
ApJohn	*Apocryphon of John*
ApThom	*Apocalypse of Thomas*
Bart	*Gospel of Bartholomew*
Clem	*Clement of Alexandria (Stromateis)*
Clem2	*Second Epistle of Clement*
EA	*Epistula Apostolorum*
James	*Apocryphon of James*
John	*Gospel of John* (NT) *
KP	*Kerygmata Petrou*
Luke	*Gospel of Luke* (NT) *
Mark	*Gospel of Mark* (NT) *
Mary	*Gospel of Mary*
Matt	*Gospel of Matthew* (NT) *
PeterE	*Apocalypse of Peter* (Ethiopic)
PeterG	*Apocalypse of Peter* (Gnostic)
Philip	*Gospel of Philip*
Rev	*Book of Revelation* (NT) *
Savior	*Dialogue of the Savior*
Seth	*Second Treatise of the Great Seth*
Sophia	*Sophia of Jesus the Christ*
Soul	*Exegesis on the Soul*
Thomas	*Gospel of Thomas*
ThomC	*Book of Thomas the Contender*
Titus	*Epistle of Titus, The Disciple of Paul*

* The following versions of the Holy Bible were consulted for the sayings of Jesus found in the New Testament (NT).

21st Century King James Version
American Standard Version
Douay-Rheims Bible
English Standard Version
Holman Christian Standard
King James Version
Lexham English Bible
New American Bible
New American Standard
New Century Version
New International Reader's Version
New International Version
New King James Version
New Living Translation
New Revised Standard
Revised Standard Version
The Darby Translation
The Living Bible
The New Jerusalem Bible
The New Oxford Annotated Bible
The Webster Bible
Third Millennium Bible
Today's New International Version
World English Bible
Wycliffe Bible
Young's Literal Translation Bible

Appendix B: Cross References

Christ Sutras (CS) is organized into numbered chapters and verses unique to itself. The following table shows the original sources for each CS verse. The source abbreviations correspond to the texts listed in Appendix A. Multiple sources are shown when a CS verse contains sayings from more than one source text or more than one place in a single source, and when multiple sources contain versions of the same saying.

The numbering system for some of the apocrypha texts is not specific enough to isolate individual lines or quotes, so the section in which the quote appears is cited. For some apocrypha texts, there is no consistent numbering system.

CS Verse	Source
1.1 - 1.7	Sophia 84:13 - 95:19
2.1 - 2.2	Thomas 18
2.3	Philip 64:11-13
2.4	John 7:28-29
2.5	John 4:25-26
2.6	Rev 1:17-18
2.7	Rev 1:8
2.8 - 2.9	Thomas 61
2.10 - 2.11	Matt 6:22-23; Luke 11:33-36
2.12 - 2.13	EA 19
2.14	Bart IV 65
2.15	EA 17
2.16 - 2.18	EA 21
2.19	John 8:58; Matt 28:18; John 10:30
2.20	Philip 67:30-35
2.21	John 14:6-7
2.22	Thomas 108
2.23	Bart I 1:5
2.24	Thomas 51
2.25	Thomas 84
2.26	Thomas 83
2.27	Mary 7:3-10
2.28 - 2.29	Sophia 98:1-10; Sophia 97:19-24
2.30	Thomas 62, 1
2.31	Thomas 42; ThomC 139:22
2.32	John 8:12
2.33	Titus
2.34	Thomas 17
2.35 - 2.36	Thomas 111, 59
2.37 - 2.38	Thomas 77
3.1 - 3.2	Matt 7:13-14

3.3	Thomas 5
3.4	James 7:18-23
3.5 - 3.6	Luke 11:9-10; Thomas 94
3.7	Savior 126:14-17, 126:8-11
3.8	Thomas 2
3.9 - 3.14	ThomC 138:4-21
3.15	Luke 10:23-24
3.16	EA 25
3.17	Thomas 17
3.18	Thomas 112, 87
3.19	Savior 141:15-20
3.20 - 3.21	Thomas 56, 80; Philip 74:30-35; Savior 141:9-13
3.22	Mark 8:34-36
3.23	John 12:25
3.24 - 3.26	EA 19
3.27 - 3.29	Thomas 3
3.30	Clem2 12:1-2
3.31	Thomas 106
3.32	Thomas 22
3.33	Luke 17:20-21
3.34	Thomas 113
3.35 - 3.36	Thomas 11
3.37 - 3.38	John 3:3; John 3:5-8;
3.39 - 3.40	Mark 10:14-15, 9:37; Matt 19:13-14; Luke 18:16-17
4.1 - 4.2	Thomas 92
4.3 - 4.5	James 14:5-20
4.6	EA 36; John 8:47
4.7	John 6:28-29
4.8 - 4.9	EA 24
4.10	Matt 11:29-30; Thomas 90
4.11	Matt 4:19, 8:22; Mark 1:17
4.12 - 4.13	John 14:21, 14:14-15
4.14 - 4.16	Mark 12:29-31; Matt 4:7, 4:10, 22:37-40; Luke 4:12, 4:8
4.17 - 4.18	Thomas 25; John 13:34-35, 15:12, 15:17
4.19	Thomas 6
4.20	John 6:27
4.21 - 4.23	Matt 6:25-26, 6:33-34; Thomas 36
4.24 - 4.25	Matt 6:27-30
4.26 - 4.27	Matt 6:31-32, 6:34
4.28 - 4.32	Luke 6:27-34; Matt 5:46-48
4.33	Luke 12-15
4.34 - 4.35	Luke 12:33-34; Matt 6:19-20
4.36 - 4.38	Matt 7:9-12; Luke 11:11-13
4.39 - 4.40	Matt 6:5-6; Philip 68:10-12
4.41	Matt 6:7-8
4.42 - 4.44	Luke 18:10-14
4.45 - 4.47	Matt 6:1-4; Thomas 62
4.48 - 4.52	Luke 10:30-37
4.53 - 4.54	Luke 14:12-14
4.55 - 4.57	Luke 14:8-11; Matt 23:12

4.58 - 4.59	Matt 6:16-18
4.60 - 4.63	Thomas 95; Luke 6:35-38; Matt 7:1-2; Mark 4:24; John 8:7
4.64	Matt 6:14-15
4.65	Luke 6:41-42; Matt 7:3-5; Thomas 26
4.66 - 4.68	EA 48-49
4.69 - 4.72	Matt 18:15-17; Luke 17:3-4
4.73 - 4.77	EA 47
4.78	John 13:15-17
4.79 - 4.80	Matt 7:24-27; Luke 6:46-49
4.81 - 4.82	Matt 5:19
4.83	James 13:2-8
4.84	James 2:29-34, 9:19-24
4.85 - 4.86	John 16:12-14
4.87	Savior 142:12-16
4.88	Matt 4:17
4.89	James 7:12-23
5.1 - 5.4	Luke 6:20-23; Matt 5:3-12; Thomas 54, 68, 69; Soul 135:17-19; ThomC 145:4-6
5.5	Thomas 49
5.6	Mary 10:15-16
5.7	ThomC 145:6-9
5.8	ThomC 145:1-3
5.9	Luke 11:28; Thomas 58
6.1 - 6.2	John 3:16-17
6.3 - 6.4	John 5:19-21
6.5	Mark 14:62
6.6	John 7:16
6.7 - 6.8	John 12:44-47
6.9	Luke 9:55-56
6.10	Mark 2:17; Matt 9:12-13; Luke 5:31-32
6.11	Luke 10:22
6.12	John 6:40
6.13	John 5:24
6.14	John 5:22-23
6.15	John 6:38-39
6.16	John 5:30-31
6.17 - 6.18	John 8:14-16
6.19	John 5:39-40
6.20	John 8:23
6.21	John 8:18
6.22	John 5:41
6.23	John 8:54-55
6.24	John 8:42-43
6.25	John 8:38
6.26	Thomas 91
6.27	John 6:62-64
6.28 - 6.29	ActsJohn 92
6.30	Thomas 29
6.31	John 8:49-51
6.32 - 6.33	James 3:1-17

6.34	John 8:19
6.35 - 6.38	John 14:9-14
6:39	John 6:35; John 6:48
6.40	John 6:51
6.41	John 7:37-38
6.42	John 4:13-14
6.43	John 4:10
6.44	John 11:25-26
6.45 - 6.46	EA 28; Titus
6.47	Matt 20:28; Mark 10:45; Luke 19-10
6.48	John 3:14-15; John 12:32
6.49 - 6.50	John 8:26-29
6.51	Luke 4:18-19
6.52 - 6.53	Luke 17:24-25; John 1:51
6.54	James 14:38-15:6
6.55 - 6.56	John 6:44
6.57	Luke 21:33
6.58	Luke 17:22-23
6.59	Matt 8:20; Thomas 86
7.1	Thomas 23
7.2	John 15:16
7.3 – 7.5	James10:27-11:7;
7.6	John 9:4-5
7.7	John 12:36
7.8 – 7.9	EA 39
7.10	James 13:18-26
7.11 – 7.12	James 12:32-13:1; John 20:29
7.13	EA 29
7.14 – 7.15	EA 19:7
7.16	John 8:31-32
7.17	Thomas 99
7.18 – 7.19	Thomas 101
7.20 – 7.21	Thomas 55; Luke 14:26-27
7.22	Mark 10:29-31
7.23	Luke 9:62
7.24 - 25	Matt 20:25-27; Luke 22:25-26
7.26 - 27	John 13:13-15; Mark 9:35
7.28	Luke 22:27
7.29	Matt 10:24
7.30	Mark 9:1
8.1	Savior 140:12-15
8.2	Clem III
8.3	Thomas 15
8.4	Bart II 7
8.5	Thomas 114
8.6	Phil 64:2-6
8.7 – 8.12	Luke 7:44-48; Mark 14:20-21
9.1	PeterE 15
9.2	Matt 6:9-13; Luke 11:2-4
9.3 – 9.4	Savior 121:5-122:1

9.5 – 9.6	Matt 11:25-27; Luke 10:21
9.7 – 9.8	Mark 11:24-26
9.9	John 16:23
9.10	John 11:41-42
9.11	Bart IV 70
10.1	Sophia 91:22-23
10.2	Luke 14:34-35; Matt 5:13; Mark 9:48-50
10.3	Mark 16:15; Luke 9:60; Thomas 42
10.4 – 10.5	Matt 13:15-17
10.6	Matt 28:19-20
10.7 – 10.8	Thomas 50
10.9 – 10.13	Bart III 66-68; Matt 7:6; Thomas 93
10.14 – 10.16	Matt 10:17, 5:14-16; Thomas 32, 33; Mark 4:21-23
10.17 – 10.20	Luke 10:3-6, 9:3-5; Mark 6:10-11; Matt 10:14-15, 10:18-13
10.21 – 10.24	Thomas 14; Mark 7:14-16, 7:18-23; Matt 15:11, 15:17, 15:19-20
10.25	EA 41:1; EA 30:7
10.26	EA 19:4-7
10.27	EA 46
10.28	Matt 10:5-7
10.29	EA 30:3-6
10.30 – 10.31	Matt 23:8-11
10.32 – 10.33	Matt 10:40-42
10.34 – 10.35	Mark 9:38-41
10.36	EA 30
10.37 – 10.38	PeterE 14
10.39	EA 41
10.40 – 10.42	EA 42
10.43	EA 32
10.44 – 10.45	Mary 8:13-9:5
10.46	John 20:21-23
10.47 – 10.48	Luke 10:19-20
10.49 – 10.51	EA 18:2-19:4
11.1 – 11.2	Matt 13:57; Luke 4:24; Thomas 31
11.3	John 15:18-19
11.4 – 11.5	John 15:20-22
11.6	John 15:24-25
11.7	Matt 10:22-23
11.8 – 11.9	Luke 21:16-19; Matt 24:9-10;
11.10 – 11.11	Clem2 5, 2-4; Matt 10:16-21
11.12 – 11.14	Luke 12:4-7, 12:8-9; Matt 10:29-33
11.15 – 11.20	Luke 12:10-12, 21:12-15; Matt 10:16-21, 12:31-33; Mark 13:9-11
11.21 – 11.24	EA 38
11.25	John 16:1-3
11.26	EA 36
12.1 – 12.7	ThomC 140:9-37
12.8 – 12.11	ThomC 141:3 — 19
12.12 – 12.20	ThomC 143:9-144:2
12.21	PeterE 16
12.22	Matt 16:23-24; Mark 8:33
12.23 – 12.27	Mark 9:42-46, 9:47-50; Matt 5:29-32, 18:3-7; Luke 17:1-2

12.28	Matt 18:10-11
12.29	John 8:34-36; Philip 77:19
12.30	Mark 14:38
12.31 – 12.32	ThomC 144:9-20
12.33 – 12.34	Titus
12.35 – 12.41	James 11:12-12:18
12.42	James 13:9-18
12.43 – 12.44	ThomC 144:37-145:1
13.1 – 13.2	Matt 19:17; Luke 18:19-20
13.3 – 13.4	Matt 5:21-22
13.5	Matt 5:27-28
13.6 – 13.7	Matt 5:29-32
13.8 – 13.9	Mark 10:5-9
13.10	Mary 7:14-21
13.11	Clem III
13.12 – 13.13	Luke 20:34-36; Titus
13.14 – 13.15	Matt 5:33-37
13.16 – 13.20	Matt 5:38-45
13.21	Matt 19:18-21; Mark 10:19, 10:21
14.1	Matt 19:26; Luke 18:27; Mark 10:26-27, 11:22
14.2 – 14.3	Matt 18:19-20; Thomas 48
14.4	Matt 21:22; John 16:24
14.5	Luke 17:6
14.6	Matt 17:20
14.7	Mark 11:23
14.8	Mark 5:36, 9:23
14.9	John 4:48, 11:40
14.10 – 14.12	Matt 8:10-13
14.13	Matt 8:7, 9:28-30
14.14 – 14.16	Matt 9:2-6; John 5:8
14.17	Matt 8:3-4
14.18	Mark 10:52; John 5:14; Luke 7:50
14.19	Matt 15:28
14.20	Matt 9:22
14.21	Matt 14:16, 15:32
14.22	Matt 16:8-11
14.23	Matt 4:4; Luke 4:4
14.24	Matt 14:31; Luke 8:25
14.25	Matt 8:26; Mark 4:39
14.26	Matt 21:24-27
14.27 – 14.28	Matt 11:4-6
15.1	Matt 5:17
15.2	Matt 5:18
15.3	KP 5, H III 50
15.4	Thomas 85
15.5	John 6:32-33
15.6 – 15.7	John 5:44-47
15.8	Mark 12:26-27; Matt 22:31-32; Luke 20:37-38
15.9 – 15.10	John 7:21-23
15.11	Thomas 53

15.12	Mark 2:27-28; Matt 12:8
15.13	Luke 14:5
15.14	Matt 12:3-5; Luke 6:3-5
15.15	Matt 12:6
15.16 – 15.17	Matt 22:41-45; Luke 20:41-44
15.18	Thomas 52
15.19	James 6:22-31
15.20	Luke 16:16
15.21 – 15.23	Matt 11:7-11; Luke 7:24-28; Thomas 46, 78
15.24 – 15.25	John 5:34-36
15.26	Matt 11:18-19
15.27	Thomas 39
15.28	Matt 23:1-4
15.29	Matt 5:20
15.30 – 15.31	Matt 17:25-27
15.32	KP 5, H III 50; Matt 22:21; Mark 12:17; Thomas 100
15.33 – 15.34	Matt 5:23-26; Luke 12:58-59
15.35 – 15.36	Luke 16:9-12
15.37	Thomas 88
15.38 – 15.45	EA 29:9
15.46 – 15.48	EA 27
16.1 – 16.4	Matt 7:15-20; EA 32:14-15; Luke 6:43-45; Thomas 45
16.5 – 16.11	Matt 24:4-5, 24:11, 24:25-28; Mark 13:5-6; Luke 17:24-25, 21:8-9; PeterE 1
16.12 – 16.15	PeterE 2
16.16	Mark 13:21-23; Matt 24:23-24
16.17 – 16.18	Matt 15:13-14; Thomas 34; Luke 6:39-40
16.19	EA 50
16.20 – 16.21	PeterG 80:24-81:3
16.22 – 16.25	PeterG 77:23-78:32, 79:23-32
16.26	EA 29
16.27 – 16.32	PeterG 73:23-75:8
17.1	Thomas 4
17.2	Matt 21:16
17.3	Matt 15:26
17.4	Philip 55:37-56:3
17.5	John 21:18
17.6 – 17.8	Thomas 47; Luke 5:36-39; Matt 9:16-17
17.9 – 17.10	Matt 12:25-29; Luke 11:17
17.11	Matt 10:25-26
17.12 – 17.13	Bart I 1:26-27
17.14 – 17.15	Mark 16:16-18
17.16	Thomas 21
17.17	Thomas 37
17.18	John 21:21-22
17.19	Thomas 7
17.20	John 7:7-8
17.21	John 15:23; Matt 12:30
17.22	Matt 19:11-12
17.23 – 17.24	Thomas 97

17.25	Philip 58:12-15
17.26	Mark 8:37
17.27	Luke 10:28
17.28	Thomas 30
17.29	Thomas 12
17.30 – 17.32	Bart III 3
17.33 – 17.34	Thomas 13
17.35 – 17.38	Matt 16:13-19
17.39 – 17.41	EA 33
17.42	Matt 17:9-12
17.43 – 17.44	PeterG 72:10-73:11
17.45	PeterG 81:29-82-3
17.46	EA 17:1
17.47	EA 50
17.48	Matt 16:23-24
17.49	Bart III 21
17.50	Matt 21:2-3
17.51	Savior 120:1-8
17.52	Thomas 60
17.53	PeterE 16; Titus
17.54	Philip 74:26-27
17.55	Philip 77:26-27, 78:12; Savior 142:7
17.56	Titus
17.57	Luke 13:2-3
17.58	John 7:24; James 8:29-30
17.59	Thomas 74
17.60	John 13:10
17.61 – 17.62	Philip 85:30-31; Clem III
17.63	Luke 12:14; Thomas 72
17.64 – 17.65	John 8:10-11; Luke 8:45-48
17.66	Thomas 105
17.67	Philip 63:26-31
17.68	Matt 26:61; John 2:19; Thomas 71
17.69	Thomas 19
17.70	Philip 72:34-73:1; Luke 24:36
18.1	Matt13:13
18.2 – 18.3	Matt 13:31-32; Mark 4:30-32; Thomas 20
18.4	Thomas 96; Matt 13:33
18.5	Thomas 109
18.6 – 18.8	Matt 13:44-46; Thomas 8, 76
18.9	Luke 14:33
18.10	Thomas 98
18.11	Luke 14:31-33
18.12	Luke 14:28-30
19.1 – 19.8	Matt 22:2-10; Luke 14:16-24; Thomas 64
19.9 – 19.11	Matt 22:11-14
20.1 – 20.2	PeterG 76:5-18;
20.3 – 20.6	John 15:1-6; Thomas 40
20.7 – 20.9	ThomC 144:20-37
21.1 – 21.2	Mark 4:3-9; Thomas 9; Matt 13:3-9

21.3 – 21.6	Matt 13:19-23; Mark 4:14-20
21.7 – 21.9	James 8:11-28
21.10	James 12:22-31
21.11	Mark 4:26-29
21.12 – 21.13	John 4:35-38
21.14	Matt 9:37-38; Luke 10:2; Thomas 73
21.15	Thomas 21
21.16 – 21.18	Matt 13:24-30; Thomas 57
21.19 – 21.22	Matt 13:37-43
21.23 – 21.24	James 7:23-26
21.25 – 21.28	PeterE 4; John 12:24
22.1 – 22.2	John 10:7-11
22.3 – 22.4	John 10:1-5
22.5 – 22.7	John 10:13-18
22.8	John 10:27-29
22.9 – 22.12	EA 43:44
23.1 – 23.4	Matt 25:1-13
23.5	Thomas 104
23.6	Matt 9:15
23.7	Thomas 75
23.8 – 23.11	EA 42-43
24.1 – 24.7	Luke 16:19-31
24.8 – 24.11	Luke 12:16-22
24.12	Thomas 81, 110
24.13	Thomas 27
24.14	Matt 19:23-24; Mark 10:25
25.1	Matt 6:24; Luke 16:13; Thomas 47
25.2	Mark 13:34
25.3 – 25.8	Luke 12:42-48; Matt 24:45-51
25.9 – 25.19	Matt 13:12, 25:14-30; Luke 19:12-27; Mark 4:25; Thomas 41
25.20	Clem2 8, 5
25.21	PeterG 83:16-84:12
25.22 – 25.25	Matt 21:33-41; Thomas 65
25.26 – 25.27	Luke 17:7-10
25.28 – 25.29	Luke 12:35-38
25.30 – 25.37	Matt 20:1-16
25.38 – 25.41	Luke 16:1-8
26.1 – 26.9	Luke 15:11-32
26.10 – 26.12	Luke 15:4-7; Thomas 107; Matt 18:12-14
26.13 – 26.14	Luke 15:8-10
26.15 – 26.16	Luke 7:41-43
26.17 – 26.18	Matt 21:28-31
26.19 – 26.20	Luke 11:5-8
26.21 – 26.23	Luke 18:2-8
27.1	Matt 15:24; Luke 4:43
27.2	Mark 8:38
27.3	Matt 11:16-17; Luke 7:31-32
27.4 – 27.5	Luke 13:34-35
27.6	Luke 11:49-51
27.7	Luke 11:29-30; Matt 16:4

27.8   Matt 16:2-3
27.9   John 4:21
27.10 – 27.11   Matt 21:42-44; Thomas 66
27.12 – 27.14   Luke 13:6-9; PeterE 2; Philip 83:13
27.15   Matt 17:17
27.16 – 27.18   Luke 11:23-26; Matt 12:43-45
27.19   Matt 16:6
27.20 – 27.21   Luke 12:1-3
27.22 – 27.23   Matt 12:34-35
27.24   Mark 12:38-40
27.25   Matt 23:14
27.26   Matt 23:13
27.27   Matt 23:15
27.28   Matt 23:23-24
27.29   Matt 23:25-26
27.30   Thomas 89
27.31   Matt 23:27-28
27.32 – 27.33   Matt 23:29-30
27.34 – 27.35   Matt 23:16-17; Matt 23:18-22
27.36 – 27.37   Mark 7:9-13
27.38   Mark 7:6-8
27.39   Luke 16:15
27.40   Matt 21:13
27.41 – 27.42   Luke 6:24-26
27.43   Luke 11:46; Luke 11:52
27.44 – 27.45   Matt 11:21-24
27.46 – 27.47   John 8:44-46
27.48 – 27.50   James 9:24-10:7
27.51   James 10:15-22
27.52 – 27.53   John 4:22-24
27.54   Luke 24:49
27.55 – 27.56   Matt 20:18; Luke 13:33
28.1 – 28.13   ActsJohn 94-96
28.14   Luke 22:10-12; Mark 14:13-15
29.1   John 7:6, 13:7
29.2   John 7:33-34, 13:33
29.3   Matt 17:22-23; Mark 9:31; Luke 9:22
29.4 – 29.6   John 16:20-22
29.7 – 29.8   John 14:16:20
29.9 – 29.10   John 16:7-11
29.11 – 29.13   John 15:7-11
29.14 – 29.16   John 14:27-31
29.17 – 29.18   John 8:19
29.19 – 29.20   John 16:32-33
29.21 – 29.23   Luke 22:15-20; Matt 26:26-28; Mark 14:20-21
29.24 – 29.25   John 6:53-56; Philip 57:4-5
29.26   John 6:57-58
29.27 – 29.28   Luke 22:21-22; Matt 26:21, 26:24; Mark 14:20-21; John 13:21
29.29   John 13:18-19
29.30   Mark 14:27-28

29.31	John 16:15-16
29.32	Bart 1:1-2
29.33 – 29.34	Matt 20:22-23
29.35 – 29.36	John 12:26-27; Matt 26:38
29.37	John 12:35
29.38	John 11:9-10
29.39 – 29.41	EA 15
29.42	Matt 26:64
29.43 – 29.48	Mark 14:36; Matt 17:7, 26:39, 26:42, 26:45-46; Luke 9:44; John 15:13
30.1	Luke 22:48
30.2	Mark 14:48-49
30.3	John 18:11; Matt 26:52
30.4	John 18:20
30.5 – 30.6	John 7:18-19
30.7	John 10:25-26
30.8	Thomas 43
30.9	John 19:11
30.10 – 30.11	John 18:36-37
30.12 – 30.13	ActsJohn 97
30.14 – 30.15	James 14:19-32
30.16	John 20:17
30.17	James 10:7-14
30.18 – 30.31	John 17:1-26
30.32	John 19: 26-27
30.33	Luke 23:34
30.34	Luke 23:43
30.35	John 19:28
30.36	Matt 27:46; Mark 15:34
30.37	John 19:30
30.38	Luke 23:46
31.1	EA 29:9
31.2 – 31.4	EA 21
31.5	EA 24
31.6 – 31.12	ActsJohn 101
31.13 – 31.15	Thomas 28
31.16	Luke 24:38-39
31.17	Luke 24:38-39; Matt 14:27
31.18	Luke 24:46-48
31.19	Luke 24:44
31.20	EA 10
31.21	PeterG 81:16-24
31.22	PeterG 82:27-83:3
31.23 – 31.24	EA 11
31.25	Bart III 18-19
31.26 – 31.27	EA 19
31.28	John 15:26-27
31.29 – 3.30	Bart I 1:28-34
31.31 – 31.35	James 4:32-5:36
31.36 – 31.39	James 6:2-17
31.40 – 31.42	EA 39-40

31.43	James 2:22-27
32.1 – 32.2	Thomas 79
32.3 – 32.4	Thomas 16
32.5	Thomas 10; Luke 12:49
32.6 – 32.8	Matt 10:34-39
32.9	Thomas 82
32.10 – 32.11	Luke 22:36-37
32.12 – 32.13	Mark 13:7-8; Matt 24:6-8; Luke 21:10-11
32.14 – 32.16	Matt 24:15-16; Mark 13:14-16; Luke 17:31-32, 21:20-22
32.17	Mark 13:2; Matt 24:2; Luke 21:6
32.18 – 32.21	Luke 21:23-24; Mark 13:17-20; Matt 24:19-22
32.22 – 32.23	EA 37
32.24 – 32.25	Luke 17:26-30; Matt 24:37-39
32.26	Matt 24:40-41; Luke 17:34-36
32.27	Mark 13:12-13
32.28 – 32.29	Matt 24:29-30; Mark 13:24-27
32.30 – 32.32	James 3:18-39
32.33 – 32.24	Luke 19:42-44
32.35	Luke 12:39-40
32.36	Luke 21:36
32.37 – 32.38	Mark 13:28-31; Matt 24:32-35; Luke 21:29-3
33.1 – 33.7	ApThom; Luke 21:25-26
33.8 – 33.28	ApThom
33.29 – 33.34	EA 34
33.35 – 33.37	EA 36
33.38	Matt 24:14
34.1 – 34.5	EA 25-26
34.6 – 34.7	John 3:19-21
34.8 – 34.11	EA 35
34.12	EA 39
34.13 – 34.22	Matt 25:31-46
34.23	ApJohn 22:12-16
34.24	ApJohn 26:25-29
34.25 – 34.30	PeterE 4
34.31	EA 29:2
34.32 – 34.38	PeterE 5
34.39 – 34.40	Matt 19:28-30
34.41 – 34.44	Luke 13:24-30
34.45 – 34.46	Matt 7:21-23
34.47	Clem2 4,5; Titus
34.48 – 34.49	PeterE 3
34.50	John 12:48
34.51 – 34.52	EA 28
34.53	Matt 24:31
34.54	Matt 24:9-10; Mark 13:32-33
34.55	Mark 13:35-37
34.56 – 34.57	Matt 24:42-44; Rev 16:15
34.58 – 34.59	Thomas 21
34.60	Thomas 103
34.61	Luke 11:21-22

34.62 – 34.63	Thomas 35; Matt 12:28-29, 24:42-44
34.64	Luke 21:34-35
34.65	Matt 12:36-37
34.66	John 12:31
34.67	EA 49
34.68 – 34.69	Matt 13:47-50
34.70	Luke 21:27-28
34.71 – 34.72	Matt 16:27-28
34.73	Titus
35.1 – 35.5	ThomC 142:28-143:9
35.6 – 35.46	PeterE 6-13
36.1 – 36.2	Rev 1:11
36.3 - 36.5	Rev 1:17-20
36.6 – 36.27	Rev 2:1-29
36.28 – 36.47	Rev 3:1-22
36.48	Rev 22:16
36.49	Rev 4:1, 10:8
36.50 – 36.57	Rev 21:3-8, 22:7, 22:12-16, 22:20
37.1	EA 16
37.2 – 37.6	EA 13
37.7 – 37.8	EA 14
37.9 – 37.10	James 8:33-9:8
37.11 – 37.13	EA 50
37.14	EA 39
37.15 – 37.16	PeterE 14
38.1 – 38.78	Sophia (complete)
39.1 – 39.5	ActsJohn 98
39.6 – 39.9	ActsJohn 99
39.10 – 39.13	ActsJohn 100
40.1 – 40.80	Seth (complete)
41.1 – 41.3	ThomC 138:29-37
41.4 – 41.6	ThomC 138:40-139:14
41.7 – 41.11	ThomC 141:26-142:2
41.12 – 41.13	PeterG 80:9-24
41.14 – 41.16	PeterG 78:32-79:22
41.17 – 41.19	PeterG 76:19-77:22
41.20 – 41.24	PeterG 70:21-72:5
41.25 – 41.26	ThomC 142:11-19
41.27 – 41.29	PeterG 75:8-76:4
41.30	ThomC 141:26-142:2
41.31 – 41.32	ThomC 145:8-17
41.33 – 41.34	PeterG 83:16-84:12
42.1 – 42.121	*Christ Sutras*

Appendix C: History of Sources

Little is known about the origins of the New Testament gospels, or of any of the other early Christian writings, but included here are brief histories of each source text used for *Christ Sutras*.

Acts of John

The Acts of John purports to give an eyewitness account of the missionary work of John the Apostle in and around Ephesus. Scholars date it from around 180 AD. The traditional author was said to be one Leucius Charinus, a real or fictitious companion of John the Apostle, but conventionally the Acts of John are ascribed to Prochorus, one of the Seven Deacons discussed in Acts. Though it was apparently popular during the early centuries of Christianity, Acts of John was eventually rejected by the official Church and most of the existing copies were destroyed. No complete text is extant, but significant portions exist in Greek and Latin.

Apocalypse of Peter (Ethiopic)

The Apocalypse of Peter, also known as the Revelation of Peter, is believed to have been written around the middle of the 2nd century AD. It was probably in wide circulation at some point, given the frequency of quotations in other sources. Once a serious candidate for inclusion in the New Testament, it was lost to history for more the 1500 hundred years until two separate fragments were rediscovered around the turn of the 20th century. Prior to this its existence was only known through references to it in other texts.

The first fragment, written in Greek, was found in Egypt in 1886. A second, Ethiopian fragment was found in 1910. The surviving fragments comprise only a few dozen verses, but the complete text is estimated to have been about 300 lines. This work should not be confused with the Gnostic text that bears the same title, discovered at Nag Hammadi in 1945.

Apocalypse of Peter (Gnostic)

The Apocalypse of Peter discovered at Nag Hammadi is sometimes known as the Gnostic Apocalypse of Peter to distinguish it from the work by the same name described above. It was probably written around 100-200 AD, and like most of the works in that discovery it is heavily Gnostic. It is also known as the Coptic

Apocalypse of Peter, because the surviving text is in Coptic, although it is likely to have been translated from an original Greek version.

Apocalypse of Thomas

The Apocalypse of Thomas is thought to have been written around 300 AD, although so little about it is known that dating is difficult. Two extant versions exist in Latin, one short and one long, with the longer being a later development. It appears to be related to, and perhaps dependent on, the Book of Revelation, and describes how the destruction of the world and the raising of the dead will come about in the final seven days.

Apocryphon of James

The Apocryphon of James, also known by the translation of its title, Secret Book of James, claims to be a book revealed by Jesus to James the Just, and may be based on an early collection of sayings. Modern scholars gave it its title, since the original had none. It shows no dependence on other texts, and was probably written around 150-200 AD. A major theme is that one must accept suffering as inevitable.

The text was discovered at Nag Hammadi as a single, damaged manuscript that appears to be a Coptic translation from Greek, although the author claims to have written in Hebrew. The text is framed as a letter from James to someone whose name is obscured by damage to the text. The author describes Jesus answering questions and expanding on teachings some 550 days after his resurrection.

Apocryphon of John

The Apocryphon of John, also known as the Secret Book of John and the Secret Revelation of John, was probably written in the latter half of the 2nd century. Considered to be a preeminent source for the Gnostic cosmological system, it describes Jesus imparting secret knowledge (gnosis) to John the Apostle in a vision, after Jesus' death and resurrection.

It is the story of God and the creation of Man—a detailed explanation of the source of consciousness and the existential predicament of being eternal Light indwelling human life. There are four surviving Coptic manuscripts of this text—two shorter versions found in the Berlin Codex and Nag Hammadi Codex III, and two longer versions, found in Nag Hammadi Codex II and IV.

Book of Revelation

The Book of Revelation, also known simply as Revelation or Apocalypse, or by several other variations, is the final book of the New Testament. Written in Koine Greek, its title is derived from the first word of the text, *apokalypsis*, meaning *unveiling* or *revelation*. Most scholars believe it was written around 95 AD, with some dating it as early as 60 AD. It is the only book of the New Testament classified as apocalyptic literature, rather than historical or didactic, because of its extensive use of allegory, visions, symbols and prediction of future events.

Revelation appears to be an anthology of separate compositions by unknown authors, though it purports to have been written by an individual named John—who calls himself the servant of Jesus—at Patmos, in the Aegean Sea. This John is traditionally supposed to be John the Apostle, but the text gives no indication of this and modern scholars tend to believe they are not the same person.

Book of Thomas the Contender

The Book of Thomas the Contender, also known as the Book of Thomas (not to be confused with the Gospel of Thomas), was one of the New Testament apocrypha discovered at Nag Hammadi, and is thought to have been written around 200-250 AD. The title derives from a combination of the name in the book's first line, "The secret words that the Savior spoke to Judas Thomas, which I, Matthias, wrote down while I was walking, listening to them speak with one another," and a line appended to the end of the text that identifies the author as "The Contender writing to the Perfect." An interesting note is that since the scribe writing the text is named Matthias, this work may actually be the lost Gospel of Matthias.

The Book of Thomas the Contender may have originally been two separate works, one a dialogue, the other a letter. It is difficult to determine how well known or widely read it may have been, but it is generally considered to be part of the wider body of Thomas literature that was an important aspect of early Christianity.

Clement of Alexandria (*Stromateis*)

Titus Flavius Clemens (150–215 AD), known as Clement of Alexandria, was a Christian theologian who came to be regarded as a Church Father. Of his many works, three survive in full and are collectively referred to as the trilogy. *Stromateis*, the third book in the trilogy, was written around 198-203 AD.

Clement titled this work *Stromateis*, (*patchwork*, or *miscellaneous*) because it deals with a variety of matters and is less systematic and ordered than his other works. It aims at the perfection of the Christian life by initiation into complete knowledge, and was possibly intended for a more limited, esoteric readership.

Dialogue of the Savior

The Dialogue of the Saviour, one of the texts found at Nag Hammadi, is generally dated to around 150 AD, and is considered the work of multiple authors. It is heavily damaged, but the surviving fragments include portions of a dialogue between Jesus, Mary, Matthew and Judas that is primarily focused on the attainment of salvation through gnosis — perfect knowledge.

Epistle of Titus, The Disciple of Paul

The Epistle of Titus, The Disciple of Paul, on the Estate of Chastity was not rediscovered until 1896 when a Latin version dating to the 5th century was found. It probably was written much earlier but its origin and author are unknown. It stresses, as the full title suggests, a life of asceticism and chastity.

Epistula Apostolorum

Epistula Apostolorum (Latin, Letter of the Apostles) is thought to have been written around 150 AD. The earliest extant text is a Coptic manuscript from the fourth century translated from the original Greek, but the only complete copy is an Ethiopic translation that was discovered and published in the early 20th century. It is more a collection of sayings than a letter, and may have been written as an Orthodox reaction against the Gnostic gospels, which also purport to describe the secret teachings of Jesus. The preface attributes authorship to all of the apostles, which may be an effort to give the work a higher authority over other writings.

Exegesis on the Soul

The Exegesis on the Soul was part of the discovery at Nag Hammadi. The original was likely written in Greek, but only a Coptic version is extant. Some scholars date it as early as the 1st century, others as late as the 4th century. It gives an account of the spiritual path of a mythic soul, and quotes heavily from the Old Testament, as well as Greek mythology. It alludes to the soul as a woman who fell from perfection into prostitution, and who will again be elevated to her perfect original state by the Father.

Gospel of Bartholomew

A work called the Gospel of Bartholomew is mentioned in other ancient writings, but scholars are unsure if it has survived. Two works that have survived, Questions of Bartholomew, and Resurrection of Jesus Christ, are considered to be possible contenders, with most scholars agreeing that Questions of Bartholomew (used in *Christ Sutras*) is likely the actual text.

The text survives as Greek, Latin, and Slavonic manuscripts, and can be dated to around 200 AD. It is framed as a dialogue between Jesus and the apostles instigated by a series of daring questions and requests by Bartholomew. It appears to have been quite popular, judging by how well it has survived.

Gospel of John

The Gospel According to John, commonly known as the Gospel of John, is the only New Testament gospel that claims to be an eyewitness account. Most scholars date it around 90-100 AD, with some theorizing it could have been written as early as 50 AD. The text identifies the author only as an unnamed "disciple whom Jesus loved," but by the beginning of the 2nd century a tradition emerged that identified the author as John the Apostle, one of Jesus' twelve disciples.

The Gospel of John differs significantly from the other three canonical gospels, Matthew, Mark and Luke, which are so alike they are known as the synoptic gospels — the term *synoptic* coming from the Greek, meaning "seen together," or "common view." By contrast, the Gospel of John, does not include the same incidents or chronology found in the synoptics, and as early as 200 AD it was already being called the "spiritual gospel" because it told the story of Jesus in symbolic ways that differed sharply from the historical focus in the other three canonical gospels.

Gospel of Luke

The Gospel According to Luke, or Gospel of Luke, is the third and longest of the four canonical gospels, and is thought to have been written in the latter part of the 1st century. Like the other canonical gospels, the Gospel of Luke is anonymous, but authorship is traditionally attributed to Luke the Evangelist. Biblical scholars generally agree that whomever authored this work also wrote Acts of the Apostles, and that these were originally a two-volume work now referred to as Luke-Acts. It is theorized that the author of Gospel of Luke used the Gospel of Mark for his history, and the work known as Q for many of Jesus' sayings and teachings.

The Gospel of Luke is written as a historical narrative divided into three stages. The first ends with John the Baptist, the second consists of Jesus' ministry, and the third focuses on the life of the church after Jesus' death and resurrection. Certain popular parables, such as "the prodigal son," and "the good Samaritan," are found only in the Gospel of Luke.

Gospel of Mark

The Gospel According to Mark, or Gospel of Mark, is the second book of the New Testament and the shortest of the canonical gospels. There is no internal or direct evidence for its authorship, but sometime during the second century it began to be ascribed to Mark the Evangelist, who is said to have been a companion of Peter the Apostle, on whose memories it is supposedly based. It tells the story of Jesus from his baptism by John the Baptist to his death and resurrection, focusing primarily on the last week of his life.

Most contemporary scholars regard the Gospel of Mark as the earliest and most historically accurate canonical gospel, and the one that establishes the life of Jesus as a story form. It was written in Koine Greek as early as 50 AD, possibly in Rome or Syria. It is believed that the gospels of Matthew and Luke used Mark as a source document, along with Q, a collection of Jesus' sayings that scholars theorize existed at the time but that has not survived in written form.

The gospels of Matthew, Mark and Luke contain so many of the same stories, often in the same sequence using similar wording, that they are referred to collectively as the synoptic gospels — meaning, seen together. The Gospel of Mark and the other synoptic gospels are the primary source for historical information about Jesus.

Gospel of Mary

The Gospel of Mary was discovered in 1896 near Akhmim in upper Egypt in a 5th-century papyrus codex. Two other small fragments of the Gospel of Mary from separate Greek editions were
250

later found in archaeological excavations at Oxyrhynchus in lower Egypt. It was originally written in Greek sometime in the 2nd century, and is attributed to Mary of Magdala, whom some scholars consider the "thirteenth disciple."

Finding three fragments of a text of this antiquity is unusual, so scholars speculate that it was well distributed and widely read by early Christians. The extant text, which is fragmentary, consists of two parts. In the first part a dialogue unfolds between Jesus' disciples and the risen Jesus as he answers their questions concerning matter and sin. In the second, Mary relates a vision she had of Jesus in which he reveals to her things that remain hidden from the other disciples.

Gospel of Matthew

The Gospel According to Matthew, or Gospel of Matthew, is one of the four canonical gospels and the first book of the New Testament. It is one of the three synoptic gospels that tells the story of Jesus' life, ministry, death and resurrection, and like the Gospel of Luke, it is generally considered to be based on the Gospel of Mark and on the hypothetical Q source document. It is thought to have been written around 60 AD, probably in Greek, although there is some evidence that suggests an earlier Hebrew version. This work does not name its author, but it does contain a vague reference to being written by a "scribe trained for the kingdom of heaven." The tradition of attributing this work to Matthew the Apostle begins around 120 AD.

The Gospel of Matthew is considered the most Jewish of the canonical gospels, and is theorized by some to have been written as late as 100 AD by an intellectual Christian Jew for a primarily Jewish audience. It stresses the continuing relevance of Jewish law and takes great interest in showing that Jesus fulfills the laws and prophecies of the Old Testament.

Gospel of Philip

The Gospel of Philip, believed to have been written in the 2nd or 3rd century AD, was one of the ancient texts rediscovered at Nag Hammadi in 1945. The title is modern and the text makes no claim to be written by Philip the Apostle. The only connection is that Philip is the only apostle mentioned in the work.

The Gospel of Philip is most well known as an early source for the theory that Jesus was married to Mary Magdalene, stating that Jesus was Mary's *koinonos*, (Greek, *companion*) and implying an intimate relationship. Like the Gospel of Thomas and some other

Gnostic texts, it teaches salvation not as rescue from sin, but as a reunification of being. It promotes ascetic practices and celibacy, and uses the language of marriage and sexual union as a metaphor for uniting the male and female aspects of man that have become separated.

Gospel of Thomas

The Gospel of Thomas is a collection of 114 sayings of Jesus, characterized by the preamble as "secret" teachings of an esoteric nature. It is mentioned in many other early Christian texts, but no copy was thought to have survived until the discovery of a Coptic manuscript at Nag Hammadi in 1945. Since then, part of the Oxyrynchus papyri have been identified as older Greek fragments of Thomas. The introduction states that, "These are the hidden words that the living Jesus spoke and Didymos Judas Thomas wrote them down." It is therefore attributed to Thomas the Apostle, who, according to many early Christian traditions, was Jesus' twin brother. Didymos (Greek) and Thomas (Aramaic) both mean *twin*.

The Gospel of Thomas is traditionally thought to have been written between 70 and 150 AD, but there is a growing consensus among scholars that it preserves earlier traditions about Jesus than do the New Testament gospels, and may actually be the first voice of the Christian tradition, dating to the earliest beginnings of Christianity. It is commonly regarded as a Gnostic gospel, but there is little in it that would have been considered unorthodox by the early Church. It does reflect the Jewish wisdom philosophy that was embraced by the Gnostics, however, teaching that the kingdom of God is not something attained after death, but that is always here, and that it can be entered while living by those who become clear and see rightly.

Since its discovery, the Gospel of Thomas has captured the attention of scholars and spiritual seekers alike, offering new insight into the inner teachings of Jesus, and new perspective on a forgotten spiritual legacy of Christianity.

Kerygmata Petrou

Kerygmata Petrou (Greek, Proclamations of Peter) is believed to be the basic document of the Pseudo-Clementines that was incorporated into the *Recognitions* and the *Homilies* of Clement, who is identified in the texts as Pope Clement I, also known as Clement of Rome. Followers of Clement of Alexandria are known as Clementines, and those of Clement of Rome as Pseudo-Clementines. *Recognitions* and *Homilies* are religious fictions that include discourses with Peter the Apostle.

Kerygmata Petrou is thought to have been written between 80 and 140 AD. No copies are extant. The Kerygmata Petrou we have today is a reconstruction of a hypothetical text created by extracting from two extant works that are presumed to have included elements from it.

Q

The document known as Q (also Q Source, Q Gospel, or Q Sayings Gospel), is a collection of sayings of Jesus that has not survived, but is theorized to have existed prior to the writing of the earliest known gospels. It is defined as the common material found in the gospels of Matthew and Luke but not in their other presumed written source, the Gospel of Mark.

Q (short for the German *quelle*, meaning *source*) is thought to have been based on the oral tradition of the early Church, and along with Markan priority is part of the "two-source" theory in modern New Testament scholarship. No sayings in *Christ Sutras* are attributed directly to Q, but it is included in this appendix as a source because of its importance to other gospels.

Second Epistle of Clement

The Second Epistle of Clement, often referred to as 2 Clement or Second Clement, was originally thought to have been an epistle to the church in Corinth written by Clement of Rome late in the 1st century AD, though many modern scholars believe it was written anonymously and erroneously attributed to Clement. Written in Greek, it appears to be a transcript of a homily or sermon delivered verbally at an early Christian worship service, and as such is the oldest complete Christian sermon extant.

Second Treatise of the Great Seth

The Second Treatise of the Great Seth is a Gnostic gospel discovered at Nag Hammadi, dating to around the 3rd century. It is written from the first person perspective of the risen Christ and almost exclusively contains his words. The author is unknown. The name Seth, which does not appear in the text, is thought to refer to the third son of Adam and Eve, to whom, according to some Gnostics, *gnosis* was first revealed.

In this work, the ascended Christ addresses his followers on earth and describes the true (Gnostic) understanding of his life story, teachings, crucifixion, and relationship to the Father. Some of these teachings differ significantly from Orthodox views, and at times mock them. While the tone of the sermon is somewhat polemical, there are passages of poetry and grace, as well as penetrating spiritual insight.

Sophia of Jesus the Christ

The Sophia of Jesus the Christ, also called the Wisdom of Jesus Christ was discovered at Nag Hammadi in 1945 as a Coptic manuscript dated to the 4th century AD, and a few fragments in Greek from a 3rd century manuscript. The date of its writing is unknown, but some scholars believe it was written in the 1st century and closely reflects the "true recorded sayings of Jesus."

Also discovered at Nag Hammadi was the Epistle of Eugnostos, or Eugnostos the Blessed, a Gnostic work that bears such striking similarities to the Sophia of Jesus the Christ, that one appears to be based on the other. It is thought that Eugnostos is the earlier work, possibly even written during the lifetime of Jesus, and that Sophia constitutes an expanded version of it within a Christian framework. Scholars speculate that Eugnostos was written for one audience and Sophia for a different group, possibly non-Christian Gnostics already familiar with Eugnostos, but for whom Christianity was something new.

The Sophia of Jesus the Christ is considered a revelation discourse, in which the risen Christ answers disciples' questions. It is highly mystical, expounding on the creation of gods, angels and the universe, with an emphasis on metaphysical truth.

Appendix D: Glossary

This glossary contains descriptions of selected terms found in *Christ Sutras* that are not in common usage.

Abba

Abba is the transliteration of the Aramaic word for *father*. In the time of Jesus the word *Abba* would be used by a child addressing his or her father with informal familiarity, akin to the modern use of *Papa* or *Daddy*. In Jesus' day, even addressing God as *Father* was considered radically informal, so his use of the even more intimate word *Abba* when asking God to "let this cup pass from me" was notable to those present.

Aeon

In Gnostic cosmology, an *aeon* is an emanation from God, a life "separate" from God. The first aeon emanates directly from the unmanifest Absolute, and is highly charged with divine energy. Aeons can also emanate aeons, and those aeons can emanate aeons, and so forth, but each successive "generation" of aeons is imbued with proportionally less divine energy, depending on how many generations removed it is from the Source. The lowest aeons are so far removed from the Source they have forgotten it, and fall into ignorance and error.

Archon

In ancient Greece the term *archon* meant *ruler* or *lord*, and the title Archon was commonly used for the chief magistrate of a province — and by extension, any religious or governmental authority. The plural of the word, *archons*, figures prominently in Gnostic cosmology and is sometimes translated as "the Authorities." More specifically, the archons are the creators and governing forces in the material world — the Demiurge and his angels, rulers of the lower aeons. The Demiurge, known as Yaltabaoth, is the chief Archon who created all the others, the god of material Creation that stands between the human race and a transcendent God that can only be known through direct experience — gnosis.

Ennoia

In general, the Greek word *ennoia* means *thought* or *thought-form*. The term is used in a variety of ways in Gnostic cosmology, most basically as *Thought of the Father*, and is fundamental to the Gnostic explanation of Creation, the heart of which is Aristotle's idea of *Noesis Noeseos Noesis*, meaning *Thought Thinking Itself*, or more literally, *Thinking a Thought of Itself Thinking*. It can also sometimes appear as a synonym for *aeon*, or as a term meaning *earthly form*. Also, Ennoia is one of the of the names given to the Mother in the Gnostic trinity of Father, Mother, and Son. Others include Sophia and Barbelo. Other variations of *ennoia* are *epinoia* and *pronoia*, which have slightly different, more specific meanings.

Epinoia

Epinoia is a form of *ennoia* that in Gnosticism refers to God's *afterthought*, as contrasted with *pronoia* which refers to God's *forethought*. The personification of this term is Epinoia, a female deity who appears late in Creation, as an afterthought of the Father, to correct faults in the material universe. Her main function is to rectify humankind's ignorance and forgetfulness by awakening us to the knowledge of Truth. See also *ennoia* and *pronoia*.

Gnosis

Gnosis is the common Greek noun for *knowledge*. In Christian mysticism and Gnosticism, it is used to mean *self-knowledge,* which is taught to be the essential path to spiritual enlightenment. Gnostics taught that a man can be delivered from the constraints of earthly existence though a direct experience of one's True Nature as that of Soul or Spirit. *Gnosis* is both the path and the goal.

Logos

In the original Greek, *logos* has a variety of meanings and connotations, such as *plea, word, opinion, expectation, reason, speech,* and *intention*. In the Christian tradition it is usually translated as *word*, and is reserved to mean *Word of God*. It connotes God's intention and capacity to communicate with humanity, and is further used to refer to the Christ, who is the "Logos (Word) become flesh." God's Word, embodied by Christ, is said to act as a bridge between Man's ignorance and the truth of God.

Mammon

The word *mammon* is used in the New Testament to refer to greed and material wealth, especially as an object of worship and devotion. It is sometimes personified as the false deity, Mammon.

Mesotes

The *Mesotes* of Jesus, one of the more enigmatic elements of Gnosticism, points to an inner guide, the Mesotes, the medium of Jesus, that will lead one to gnosis—pure knowledge of God.

Monad

Monad is from the Greek, *monos*, meaning *single*, a symbol used by ancient Greek philosophers to describe God or the totality of all life—an elementary singular substance that reflects the order of the world and from which material properties are manifested. Metaphysical and theological theory describes *monism* as the concept of *One Essence*. In some Gnostic systems, God, the Supreme Being, is called the *Monad*, the One, the Absolute. The Monad is the source of material Creation, which emanates from the *Pleroma*, the realm of infinite light.

Nous

In ancient Greek, *nous* meant *common sense*. It is today often translated as *mind*, as well as *understanding, reason,* or *thought*. In philosophy it points to the capacity of the human mind to understand what is real or true, not through thought or senses, but through an "inner seeing." In some spiritual traditions it refers to the first emanation of God, the divine intelligence that is the source of all Creation.

Pleroma

Pleroma (Greek) means *fullness*, or *perfection*. In Christian theology it refers to the totality of the Godhead that lives in Christ. In Gnosticism, the Pleroma generally refers to the spiritual realm of God, and of the totality of the divine powers and emanations. It is contrasted with the Deficiency, which is the realm of the material universe. Carl Jung also wrote about the pleroma, calling it "both nothing and everything." He went on to say, "It is quite fruitless to think about pleroma. Therein both thinking and being cease, since the eternal and infinite possess no qualities."

Pronoia

In ancient Greek philosophy *pronoia* means *providence*, usually *divine providence*, or *destiny*. In Gnostic systems it is a variation of *ennoia* and refers to God's *forethought*, as opposed to *epinoia*, God's *afterthought*. The term is also personified as Pronoia, a female savior deity who appears early in Creation to emphasize that God's thought, or forethought, pre-exists and determines all else. See also *ennoia* and *pronoia*.

Raca

Raca is an Aramaic word derived from a root meaning *to spit*. It was used as a reproach of extreme contempt, meaning someone was *worthless, vain, foolish, empty-headed*.

Sutra

Sutra is a Sanskrit word that translates literally as *thread*. It derives from the same root and meaning as the Latin word *suere* (stitch together), the English word *sew*, and the medical term *suture*. In ancient Indian literature, *sutra* denotes a type of literary composition, usually spiritual in nature, such as *Yoga Sutras*, that consists of concise aphoristic statements intended for memorization. This usage of the word began when memorized oral teachings were first written down on palm leaves stitched together with thread into books. In Buddhism *sutra* refers to a spiritual narrative, especially those involving a discourse by Buddha. One famous definition of the form of a sutra is itself a sutra:

> *Of minimal syllables, unambiguous, pithy,*
> *comprehensive, continuous, and without flaw:*
> *who knows the sutra knows it to be thus.*